Getting
into the
Vortex

Guided Meditations CD
and User Guide

Other Hay House Titles by Esther and Jerry Hicks

(The Teachings of Abraham®)

❖

All of the above are available at your local bookstore, or may be ordered by visiting:

Hay House USA: **www.hayhouse.com®**;
Hay House Australia: **www.hayhouse.com.au**; Hay House UK: **www.hayhouse.co.uk**;
Hay House South Africa: **www.hayhouse.co.za**; Hay House India: **www.hayhouse.co.in**

Getting into the Vortex

Guided Meditations CD and User Guide

ESTHER and JERRY HICKS

(The Teachings of Abraham®)

HAY HOUSE, INC.
Carlsbad, California • New York City
London • Sydney • Johannesburg
Vancouver • Hong Kong • New Delhi

Published and distributed in the United States by: Hay House, Inc.: www.hayhouse.com • *Published and distributed in Australia by:* Hay House Australia Pty. Ltd.: www.hayhouse .com.au • *Published and distributed in the United Kingdom by:* Hay House UK, Ltd.: www .hayhouse.co.uk • *Published and distributed in the Republic of South Africa by:* Hay House SA (Pty), Ltd.: www.hayhouse.co.za • *Distributed in Canada by:* Raincoast: www.raincoast .com • *Published in India by:* Hay House Publishers India: www.hayhouse.co.in

Editorial supervision: Jill Kramer • *Project editor:* Alex Freemon • *Design:* Charles McStravick

Library of Congress Control Number: 2010934773

Hardcover ISBN: 978-1-4019-3169-8

13 12 11 10   4 3 2 1
1st edition, November 2010

Printed in the United States of America

Contents

Preface

by Jerry Hicks

If you are like most of us, you will likely want to listen to a portion of the enclosed guided-meditations CD even before settling down to read the accompanying users' guidebook.

However, with this potentially powerful means of personal life enhancement that you now have in your hands, we lovingly suggest that you first set aside about 45 minutes to acquaint yourself with the "General Well-Being" portion of the *User Guide* before proceeding to the guided-meditations recordings.

When Esther and I began creating this *Getting into the Vortex Guided Meditations CD* and accompanying *User Guide* package, our intention was to create a first-of-its-kind user-friendly tool that would facilitate the user's Vibrations to a better-feeling place in four basic areas: the feeling of *General Well-Being* and the feelings and perspectives regarding *Financial Abundance, Physical Well-Being,* and *Relationships.*

Please note that neither the guided-meditations CD nor the information in the accompanying *User Guide* is intended to replace any professional psychological or medical assistance, but rather to be used to augment any other means of feeling better that the listener might be currently utilizing.

Abraham has taught us (from the beginning of our interaction over two decades ago) that anything we intend to do (whether others may judge our intentions as *good* or *bad*) . . . is only because we believe that in the achieving of it, *we* will feel better. . . . And so, these Teachings of Abraham are primarily focused on simply getting into that better-feeling place (the Vortex) right now!

We would advise that you learn to use Abraham's recordings in whatever ways feel best to you, but we don't recommend that you meditate for more than 15 minutes per day. . . . As Abraham advises, "Life is for conscious, aware, joyous *living;* and so, 15 minutes of daily meditation is quite enough." Also, the respiratory tempo of the guiding musical tones (which are intended to help you remember to deeply breathe) will likely feel extremely slow as you begin this process. If so, we suggest that (rather than trying to force it) you, over a period of days, or even weeks, simply allow your breathing pattern to gently but naturally relax into the soothing, life-enhancing tempo of six breaths per minute.

We definitely do not advise that you listen to Abraham's relaxing meditation recording while driving a vehicle. (There are hundreds of other Abraham recordings that are ideal for drive-time listening.) And, unless you *want* to fall asleep, we would suggest that you enjoy the daily-meditation recording while seated upright (with your eyes closed to avoid any distraction).

By the way, all Teachings of Abraham® are copyrighted by Jerry and Esther Hicks, and we are most appreciative of whatever your role may be in expanding the availability of this delicious co-creative experience. And so, should you decide to share this material with others, we want to ask you (in advance) to share it in its purest and most valuable form—and that would be to give them access to both this *Getting into the Vortex User Guide* and the enclosed guided-meditations CD.

For a better understanding of our teacher, Abraham; or of who we, Jerry and Esther, are; or to receive additional materials from our massive library of books, catalogs, CDs, and DVDs—or even to reserve space at an Abraham-Hicks *Vortex of Attraction* cruise or workshop— please visit our interactive Website at **www.abraham-hicks.com**, or call our office at (830) 755-2299.

So, after over two decades of studying with Abraham, I only recall three things that Abraham has ever taught us regarding maintaining, or improving, our physical well-being: Number 1—*Think more good-feeling, in-the-Vortex thoughts.* Number 2—*Drink more water.* And Number 3 (and it's a major theme of these daily guided meditations)— *Breathe more deeply.*

So now, let's get started. Esther is going to ask Abraham to guide us into the process for most effective utilization of the guided-meditations CD. And so, plan on getting comfortable and sitting back, relaxing, and closing your eyes while taking a deep breath, as you allow Abraham to lovingly and gradually guide you into the joyous, life-enhancing Vortex of your natural state of Well-Being.

⋇ ❀ ⋇ ⋇ ❀ ⋇

(**Editor's Note:** Please note that since there aren't always physical English words to perfectly express the Non-Physical thoughts that Esther receives, she sometimes forms new combinations of words, as well as using standard words in new ways—for example, capitalizing them when normally they wouldn't be—in order to express new ways of looking at old ways of looking at life.)

Introduction

by Abraham

It is nice to have an opportunity to visit about the subject of this recording, for it has been created especially to help you in the following way: When you are in a state of *allowing,* which means you have quieted your mind—or focused your mind in such a way that there is an absence, or a decreasing, of resistant thought—your Vibration naturally rises. Now, what that means is, you are coming closer and closer to Vibrational alignment with *who-you-really-are,* to the frequency of your Source, and to the frequency of your *Inner Being*—and under those Vibrational-alignment conditions, you must thrive. And so, our recording has been devised with the intent that you might set aside 15 minutes each day where—as you simply listen and relax and breathe—you will naturally come into a different Vibrational state.

So you will be, so to speak, training your Vibration *away* from patterns of resistance and *toward* patterns of allowing, which will make it, over time, just natural for you to find those better-feeling thoughts. When you find better-feeling thoughts and when you release resistance, your natural Vibration rises; and when your natural Vibration rises, you will have achieved a different and improved point of attraction. And so, now, that different point of attraction brings you better-feeling things to observe—and your life just gets better and better.

Our recording is called *Getting into the Vortex Guided Meditations CD,* and what that literally means is focusing your mind upon the thoughts that allow your alignment with the broader part of *who-you-really-are.* And *who-you-really-are,* from our perspective, is already *in* the Vortex.

Whenever you know what you *do not* want, there is an equivalent awareness of what you *do* want, an awareness (at some level) sometimes not even conscious to you—an awareness that radiates from you, like a rocket of desire, into what we are calling a *Vortex of Creation. Your* Vortex of Creation. So as that desire, which you have carved out of the life that you are living, moves forward Vibrationally into this Vibrational place that we are calling a Vortex of Creation, *the <u>Law of Attraction</u> (the essence of that which is like unto itself, is drawn) then draws all cooperative components to it.*

Anytime you are feeling negative emotion—or anytime your experience is diminished in any way—it is only because you, in your physical form, because of your physical thought, are not Vibrationally up to speed with this expanded version of you. Our meditation recording is designed to assist you in getting up to speed with *you* and to help you be consistently a Vibrational Match to that furthermost expanded part of you. When you find a way to stop resisting *who-you-have-become*—and to allow yourself to become a Vibrational Match to *who-you-have-become*—you are in the Vortex, and you are in a state of thriving.

Everything that we teach really is about helping you move in the direction of what feels better, but our recording has been specifically created in order to assist you in understanding this very important thing: *Anytime you try hard—from your position of need or pain or concern or worry or anger or hurt, from outside the Vortex—there is a very strong probability that your attempt, your effort, your struggle, your work . . . is completely counterproductive, because it just amplifies the outside-the-Vortex pattern that you already have going.*

If you can find a way of focusing differently so that you find yourself inside the Vortex, in alignment with <u>who-you-really-are,</u> and then, from inside the Vortex, you do 100 percent of your affirming, it is a shortcut that we think is really worth considering. And that is what our meditations user guide/CD is really all about. It is a faster way for you to release resistance, some of it that you have been carrying around for most of your life. It is a faster way of using the leverage of the Energy that creates worlds to help you to get from where you are to the improved state of being that you prefer.

As you move forward with the different segments of the recording, you will find them to be beneficial no matter where you begin. Our encouragement is that you begin, on your first listening, with the segment entitled "Meditation: General Well-Being"; and then progress, as the CD has been laid out for you, into the segment on "Financial Abundance," then to the segment on "Physical Well-Being," and then to the segment on "Relationships."

If you will listen to the recordings in that order for the first week—and then, in the subsequent weeks, just choose any part that you feel inspired to—it is our absolute expectation that the Vibrational patterns that you have developed will gradually begin to shift, and your point of attraction will improve.

There is nothing of greater advantage to you—or that links you more powerfully with the Source from which you have come—than that of your breathing. As you listen to the recording in an attitude of gentle ease—and as you make some small effort to breathe as the music guides you—your physical body will benefit. And as you do it consistently (every day for a week or so) at least for the time that you are listening to the recording, you will enter your Vortex. And it is also our powerful knowing that once you are inside your Vortex—in utter alignment with *who-you-really-are* while you are hearing the powerful words that we are speaking gently in your ear—you will tune yourself completely to the frequency of your Source. And under those conditions, from *inside* your Vortex of Creation, you will not only align with the power of your Being, with the clarity of your intentions, with the purpose of your existence, and with the worthiness of that which is you, but all things that you have been asking for will now be *allowed* to show themselves to you. And so, this will be an exercise of great fun.

Consistency is of value. If you will sit for 15 minutes every day once you are under way with this—wearing comfortable clothing, sitting in a comfortable space, closing your eyes, and focusing on your breathing as you hear the words of empowerment—you will return to *who-you-are.*

There is great love here for you. And, as always, we remain—in the Vortex.

Meditation:
General Well-Being

Welcome to the doorway of your Vortex.
We are extremely pleased that you have made
the decision to be here. It is good to come together
for the purpose of co-creation and for the purpose
of aligning with *who-you-really-are.*

Even though this Vortex that we speak of cannot be found on physical maps and is not indicated by physical signposts, it is a reality that exists just the same. It is your Vibrational Reality.

You can tell when you enter your Vortex by the way you feel. You can tell by the way you feel when you exit your Vortex. In fact, your personal, precise *Emotional Guidance System* is the only effective road map or signpost to your Vortex.

Your Vortex is a Vibrational haven where the frequencies are very high and without resistance. That is why it feels so good to you when you enter. And that is also why we are extremely pleased that you have made the decision to be here.

All cooperative components to the furthermost expanded version of you have been gathered by the *Law of Attraction* and are held in timeless, spaceless ever readiness, for your access and utilization in your Vortex of Creation.

If you are to become a cooperative component to your own Vortex and to all of the wonderful things that have been gathered there, you must be a Vibrational Match to your Vortex. In other words, you too must have a high frequency, and you too must be without resistance.

Each day, as you release resistant thoughts—through the power of this guided meditation—your Vibrational frequency will rise and new Vibrational patterns will develop until, in a short period of time, your natural Vibrational inclination will be to be inside your Vortex. And then, you will be living life as you intended to live it, accessing the Energy that creates worlds and flowing it toward your personal creative endeavors—for you are the Creator of your own reality.

We want you to know that as you relax
and breathe and focus softly upon the words
that we are offering to you here, you are allowing
the gentle tuning of your Vibration to the frequency
of your Source, who is inside the Vortex.

There is nothing about your physical awareness that connects you more to the Non-Physical aspect of your Being than that of your breathing.

Many assume that the process of breathing is only about your physical nature, but that is not the case. *The process of breathing is much more than an essential function of your physical body. Indeed, it is the flowing of Spirit to you, and through you.* That is the reason that when the focusing of Spirit through your physical body ceases, your breathing ceases, also.

When you are in a state of complete alignment and no resistance is present within you, the absence of any negative emotion is your indication of your complete alignment with Source.

This listening experience will induce a convergence of beneficial aspects for you, for as you relax into the natural rhythm of perfect breathing while hearing these spoken words, the Vibration of your physical being will gently surrender to the Vibrational frequency of your Source, and you will become one with your Source, inside the Vortex.

Over time, by focusing upon your breathing while hearing the perspective of Source in the background, the resistant thoughts you have picked up along your physical trail will be released, and your natural alignment with the Source within you will return. Through the hearing of these words in your relaxed state of allowing, you will allow the gentle tuning of your Vibrational frequency to match the frequency of your Source.

This will not be an exercise of effort or trying, but instead an exercise of releasing and allowing . . . gently allowing yourself to be <u>who-you-really-are.</u>

⋅{ 3 }⋅

Be easy as you find the rhythm of your body; and enjoy long,
slow breaths, in and out, as you hear our words.
It is not necessary that you concentrate,
and there is nothing that you need remember;
just relax and breathe and enjoy.

The key to the certain benefit that you are discovering here is in
the distraction from resistant thoughts that are often present. Because
of the subtle rhythm implied here in the music at the basis of this
recording, your early attention will be upon that, assuring a releasing
of your normal resistant thoughts and concerns.

As you listen for the rhythm of the music and gradually align your
breathing in and out with that gentle rhythm, your body will thrill
with the discovery of optimal breath and Non-Physical alignment.

In this moment in time and space,
you are precisely where you have intended to be,
and the Source within you is pleased—for your life
continually calls more expansion through you, and
All-That-Is benefits from the important part that you play.

When your life presents a situation where a clear new question
within you, you are moving into new expansion. And even
the answer to your question seems nonexistent, you are still
ong the way to personal growth.
en you stand in the middle of a problem, or even what you
ard as a crisis, you are also moving into new expansion. And
ough the solution to your problem feels out of reach to you,
ver the case.

Full, strong breath *in* . . . 1, 2, 3 . . . and a long, slow, easy breath *out* . . . 4, 5, 6, 7, 8. And, in time, after a few days of refreshing yourself in this way, your body will remember its newfound rhythm, your awareness of your breathing will gently become unconscious, and your physical body will delight in this physical experience of relaxing enjoyment.

Then, while in that subtle unconscious state of being, the words you have been hearing in the background will move forward in your awareness in a new and powerful way. And in your quiet state of nonresistance, you will feel a Vibrational resonance with the understanding that is at the basis of these words.

This will not be a process of hearing and then remembering so that you can repeat these words, but an awareness, as you hear them, that you *know* them.

Within this process, you will come to understand, firsthand, the state of Universal Well-Being in which you live: a state where effort and trying are replaced with relaxing and allowing . . . a state where worthiness is not earned, but simply accepted.

You are an extension of Non-Physical Source Energy,
and you have come here with great eagerness and purpose.
You intended to explore Earth's perfect balance
of contrast for the purpose of moving
life beyond what it has been before.

You are an Eternal Being, a part of which is now focused into the physical body that you believe is you, but your physical person and personality are only part of *all-that-you-really-are.*

We like to explain that *only a part of the Consciousness that is really __who-you-are__ is focused into the physical personality that you believe is you,* so that you can then begin to consciously consider the larger part of you, who continues to remain Non-Physically focused.

Once you remember that you are a physical extension of Source Energy, you can then begin to consider, and consciously tend to, your alignment with your larger, Eternal, Non-Physical counterpar

As you made the decision to focus into this physical time-spa reality, you understood it to be a spectacular arena of balance variety and perfect contrast.

You felt eager about the promise of opportunities that offered. You knew that your experience here would evoke co preferences and decisions and expansion.

You felt eager about what you knew would be a det sure to experiences and people and ideas from whic preferences of creation would be born.

You understood that there is no competition for res opportunities to give birth to your own ideas—and yo once an idea has been given birth, the means with w follow.

And now here you are, an extension of Sou in the environment of perfect contrast and have intended—exploring, deciding, pre becoming.

Whenever any question or problem is coming into focus in your life—an equivalent answer or solution is coming into focus as well.

From your Non-Physical perspective, as you were making the decision to focus into your physical body, you understood completely this amazing process of creation and expansion, and you eagerly set forth your intention to be here at this time and in this space. You reveled in the idea of continual rendezvous with other creators, and you understood that you would be catalysts for one another for joyous expansion.

As your life continually poses new questions, it also poses new answers—which cause expansion. As your life presents new problems, it also presents new solutions—which cause expansion—and *All-That-Is* benefits from your willingness to live and consider and explore . . . and expand.

Because the Source within you is so aware of this process (understanding the certainty of the answers and solutions), every part of your physical exploration is joyously appreciated.

Through this process, you will return to your Non-Physical understanding, and then problems will cease to be problems and will be seen for what they really are—life-giving opportunities for Eternal expansion.

As you relax and breathe deeply,
you can feel the appreciation that Source feels for you
in this moment in time—appreciation for your physical world,
for its diversity, and for the stream of never-ending
desires that flow forth from you.

The Non-Physical Source from which you have come is always aware of you, always enjoying you, always loving you, and always feeling appreciation for the important role you are playing in the expansion of *All-That-Is.* Your lack of awareness of the Source within you in no way hinders the ability of Source to be aware of *you.*

Since your Non-Physical Source Energy is always aware of you, always flowing to you, any disruption in that communication is always caused by <u>you</u> because of whatever you are focused upon in that moment *in time. But, day by day, as you give your attention to the rhythm of the guiding music, to the cadence of your breathing, to the feeling of these words—any long-held patterns of resistance will dissipate.*

Since resistance that has been introduced by your thoughts is the only thing that hinders the conscious blending between you and your *Inner Being,* as that resistance gradually dissipates, your conscious awareness of your relationship with Source will come forward into your awareness.

When you feel love or appreciation or passion or joy, those feelings are not only your indication that you are blended with the Source within you, but they are also indicators of how Source is also feeling. Because of the perspective of love that Source always chooses to hold, there is always a guiding Vibrational signal for you to tune yourself to.

A simple withdrawal of your attention from resistant thoughts is the only path to your alignment with the pure, positive Energy that is at your core. And so, just relax and breathe deeply, and allow your natural alignment.

Before your birth into this physical body,
you understood the importance of the contrasting
diversity on planet Earth. You jumped in eagerly to explore
the variety and to enjoy the expansion that you knew
would be called through you.

From your physical point of view, you understand how appealing a variety of choices and opportunities can be as you are choosing your food, your clothing, your vehicles, your homes, your relationships. . . . You know that the more options that are available, the more satisfying your experience is, because more options allow more detailed creativity.

From your Non-Physical point of view, you hold an even greater appreciation for variety and contrast, because not only does contrast make for more satisfying choices—but it is the basis of all new creation.

It is far more than observing the varied offerings like in a buffet and simply selecting the components to create a satisfying plate. Instead, it is the satisfying understanding that the existing components will continue to produce a never-ending plethora of new components from which to choose. The dynamics of creation are intoxicating and life-giving.

In your understanding of the creative process and of the important role that you would play in the expansion of *All-That-Is,* you eagerly jumped into this time-space. You were eager to explore the options that had been created by those who had come before you. You were eager to explore, and to observe and to evaluate and to decide. But the eagerness you felt was not only about having an opportunity to observe the existing components that had been created before your arrival. Your eagerness was about the creativity that would flow out of you as you digested what was there and discovered your new personal requests for more. . . . *The Leading Edge of thought and of creation—that is where you wanted to be.*

Your life is supposed to feel good to you,
for you have deliberately chosen it as the platform
from which more will flow. The appreciation that
Source feels for you, never-endingly, will wrap you
in a warm blanket of worthiness if you will allow it.

As you were coming into your physical experience, you understood that the basis of the Universe—both physical and Non-Physical—is one of absolute Well-Being.

You felt no concern about the existence of unwanted things, since you understood the importance of contrast and variety, and you knew that more wonderful creation would be born from that variety.

You knew that your emphasis and focus would be upon the new creation that would be born from the variety, and therefore the contrast that spawned the expansion was a good thing.

...ng and sifting through the details of wanted and ...gives birth to constant new rockets of desire. ...to redirect your focus from your awarenes... ...desirable aspects of your observation, toward th... ...ion that are born out of that very observation, yo... ...me Vibrational wavelength as the Source within you, ... looks forward to the newest of creation.

In your redirection of y... ...sonal focus toward the new idea that has been launched, you ... ...lend with the Leading Edge perspective of Source, and you w... ...l your at-oneness with *who-you-really-are* and with *all-that-you*... *-become.*

When no Vibrational resist... *is hindering the communication between you and your Source, you will feel the visceral, tactile feeling of your Vibrational alignment with the Source within you. And while physical words are inadequate to describe the physical sensation, every cell of your body will confirm your alignment with Source inside the Vortex.*

Your life is serving you well and is providing
the basis of expansion, exactly as you knew it would
when you decided to come, for you have launched
countless rockets of desire into your Vortex of Creation,
and your frequent entry there will always feel good.

All day, every day, contrast—in varying degrees—is causing you to launch rockets of desire into your Vortex of Creation. Sometimes the contrast is such that you launch what feels like very big requests, and sometimes the rockets feel as if they are simply amending previous intentions. And so, your expansion never ceases . . . because your rockets never cease . . . because the contrast never ceases.

When a new desire is born from contrast, Source always feels the pleasing experience of expansion, because Source holds no resistance to the new expansion, and therefore experiences the expansion immediately.

The purpose of our recording is to assist you in the gentle and progressive releasing of practiced resistance, which will allow you to frequently enter your Vortex.

Every time you allow your entry into your Vortex, you will feel good, because every time you enter, you will align with your own expansion.

And so, the contrast that surrounds you will always assure your expansion. . . . And the Source within you will always focus upon that expansion. . . . And your releasing of unpleasing thoughts will allow your good-feeling entry into your Vortex, where you are a cooperative component to the desires that you hold.

Through your gentle and progressive releasing of resistance, and your frequent entry into your good-feeling Vortex, not only will it become increasingly easy for you to remain there longer—but it will be infinitely easier for you to return to your Vortex with ease.

There is no better-feeling physical sensation than what is experienced when you allow your Vibrational alignment with your Source and with your own expansion.

❧ 10 ❧

From inside your Vortex, things satisfy and delight you,
you feel expansive and frisky, and you are eager for more.
With every new discovery—and each new place you stand—
the expansive feeling of *more* continues
to call you and refresh you.

When you are outside your Vortex of Creation, focusing upon
unwanted things, equivalent ideas of *wanted* things are simultane-
ously coming into focus. Your awareness of what you *do not* want
creates a Vibrational version of what you *do* want, but you do not
have access to that wanted version while outside your Vortex. In
other words, your attention to the details of your current buffet of components is creating other components, but you do not
have access to those choices at this time. But when you are in your

Vortex, now all of those good-feeling, newly created choices are there for your choosing. In other words, while *inside* your Vortex, you are choosing from the very best that life has to offer.

So, while we always want you to feel the benefit of contrast (no matter where you stand within it), we want you to know that it is not necessary to experience discomfort in order to experience expansion. You could consistently remain inside your good-feeling Vortex and enjoy infinite choices with which to create your evolving reality.

Even when you are choosing from the good-feeling buffet from inside your Vortex, you are still creating new components, new possibilities, new ideas, and new expansion. Not only are you creating new components to mold into the details of your life experience, but you are creating a continuing new perspective from which to enjoy them. More discoveries, more relationships, more combinations, more adventures, more awareness, more desires, more appreciation. . . .

It is always that which is new that refreshes. . . . It is in that which is new where Source dwells—offering a signal of love and joy that calls you never-endingly forward to never-ending expansion. To <u>more!</u>

Your world is gradually expanding, steadily growing and
refreshing while finding balance every step along the way.
Well-Being is the dominant basis of *All-That-Is*,
of the Universe, and of the physical planet upon
which you now stand.

Your planet spins in its orbit, in proximity to other planets, in
a perfect and stable dance because it is perpetually seeking and
finding balance.

Like all living Beings, your Earth is continually changing and
expanding. Otherwise it would cease to be.

*The stability of your Earth exists because its change and expansion
does not outstrip its ability to find balance.* It is not only Earth's size
and the laws of physics that are of enough significance to absorb

the shock of any change, but also Earth's Vibrational nature of Well-Being.

While your Earth appears to be a geological sphere of rock and soil and water held together by gravitational forces, it is so much more than that, for within every particle of Earth's substance is Vibrational Consciousness seeking individual balance—Consciousness aligning with a Broader Non-Physical vision of Earth's future.

In the same way that a large ship, outfitted with modern stabilizers, sails largely unaffected in stormy seas, while earlier vessels, less well equipped, were buffeted about, your planet's evolution has guaranteed its stability. Your planet is not moving back to less stability.

Even though the human inhabitants of planet Earth are often outside of their Vortices, in a state of resisting their personal Well-Being, the overwhelming Consciousness of your planet (in soil, in water, in flora and fauna) is incrementally finding balance every step along the way.

In time, as you relax and breathe your way into alignment with your Source, you will be able to feel the dominant Vibrational pulse of Well-Being that permeates your Earth and everything it is comprised of. <u>*Well-Being is the basis of* All-That-Is.</u>

12

Your magnificent world is eternally
tied to the steady rhythm of Well-Being at its core—
and the same is true of you. As you relax and refresh,
releasing resistance as you breathe, you will discover the
balancing rhythm of your Source.

You, in your physical body, are an extension of Source Energy; and your physical planet is an extension of Source Energy, also.

You have a Non-Physical counterpart that we refer to as your *Inner Being,* and your planet has an *Inner Being* as well. Every particle of your physical world has a Non-Physical Source from which it has come, and every particle of your physical world also has a Leading Edge Vibrational version that is calling it forward.

This Vibrational version of what you could call your physical future holds a steady rhythm of Well-Being for you in your Vortex.

In the same way that the large and diverse variety of Vibrational components that make up your Earth assures its stability, the trillions of cells that make up your physical body do the same for you. That is the reason for the extraordinary resiliency of your physical body.

The unlimited Consciousness of the particles that make up your immense planet never, under any conditions, worry themselves out of alignment with the Energy of their Source. The core Vibration of Well-Being is so significant that departure from it does not occur.

Over time, during the application of this process, your habits of worry, concern, frustration, overwhelment, and anger will cease to be, allowing your cellular core to find its natural Vibrational balance. Day by day, as you relax and breathe, your natural Well-Being will dominate until your stable footing will become unshakable. Your consistent alignment with the Energy of Well-Being will cause you to see your world through the eyes of Source, and you will feel as you felt when you decided to come into your physical body: satisfied with <u>what-is</u> and eager for more!

Be easy about your life, and feel
our appreciation for *who-you-are* as you allow
wonderful things to flow naturally to you. As you relax into
the *Law*-based premise of our words, any resistance you have
found along your physical path will be released.

Because of your daily tuning to the frequency of your Source, everything in your life experience will be beneficially affected by that decision.

Be easy about your life, letting all struggles and concerns go. No longer try to *make* things happen. Release your attempted control of circumstances and others. Stop beating up on yourself. Stop measuring your progress. And when you catch yourself beginning to do any of that, remind yourself that you are taking care of everything that needs to be tended to during the daily tuning sessions you are now participating in. Then *relax* and *breathe* and *smile*—and *allow*.

Before long, you will realize that it has always been your struggle and concern—and attempt at impossible control—that has been holding unwanted things to you. With less resistance and more allowing, unwanted things cannot remain.

Before long, you will witness a steady stream of wanted things flowing into your experience with the same ease and flow of water flowing gently downhill. You will discover how simple and delightful the harvesting of desires you have already put into your Vortex is when you are consistently residing inside your Vortex.

Your Vortex will teach you, as you are consistently inside, that your best *effort* is in letting go of resistance and simply *allowing* yourself inside. For inside your Vortex, your thoughts flow with ease and clarity and precision, your physical body feels stable, your stamina is high, and your timing is perfect as you interact with others.

You will be surprised, at first, at what little effort was actually required to tune yourself to the Energy that creates worlds, and that your true power is in non-struggle.

14

As you listen to our words and remember *who-you-are*,
you will rediscover your natural Vibrational patterns
of Well-Being. Each day you will find more clarity,
more stamina, and more eagerness. Each day you will
remember *who-you-are* and why you have come.

You have picked up your Vibrational resistance to Well-Being gradually as you have been moving along your physical trail—and your releasing of this resistance will be gradual as well.

The better-and-better-feeling path to the freedom of no resistance is a progressive one, and each new day will be more productive than the day before. Therefore, a consistent listening to our recording is of tremendous value to you.

If you will make a decision to let your singular conscious intention be to focus upon your breathing, several natural benefits will begin to emerge during the first month of this daily meditation process: During your first several segments of listening to the recording, it will be normal for your mind to drift away from your attention to your breathing and on to some Vibrationally active aspect of your life. Even the words that we are speaking on the recording may stimulate a resistant thought within you. But after a few days of relaxing and breathing, you will begin to feel the ease of a quieter mind—and the process of simply breathing will begin to feel inviting and beneficial to you.

Because of your willingness to focus upon your breathing, and in doing so, to deactivate what have been resistant thoughts, the words on the recording will move into the foreground, and you will begin to feel a striking awareness of the power of these words. Not because the words are becoming clearer, but because your reception of them is becoming clearer.

Each day, you will find more clarity; more ease; more eagerness; more awareness; more vitality; more stamina; more fun; more interest; more good timing; and more harmonious rendezvous with ideas, circumstances, events, and others. Each day you will come into greater Vibrational alignment with your natural state of Well-Being.

That which is your Source is fully aware of you right now,
and feels unspeakable appreciation for *who-you-are.*
Your life is supposed to feel good to you, and
you are meant to feel happiness in your life—
and you are meant to satisfy your dreams.

The Source within you is always fully aware of you, even though you may not be fully aware of Source. And in the same way that the words on our recording are not changing and becoming clearer, but instead it is your reception that is changing and allowing the clarity— you will begin to allow your own clearer recognition of your relationship with your Source.

Unless you are in the state of alignment with the love that Source flows to you, it is as if it is not really there, when, in fact, it always is there. It is not enough to be loved by another. You must be a Vibrational Match to that love in order to know the experience of being loved.

To be in your natural state of love and appreciation does not require lovable objects for you to focus your attention toward, but only an absence of resistance, which is the only thing that can hinder or mute your natural state of love and appreciation and Well-Being.

In the absence of resistant thought, your Vibration returns to its natural state of power and clarity and love. In the absence of resistant thought, your true nature of resilience and replenishment and vitality returns. In the absence of resistant thought, your true nature of eagerness and joy and fun returns.

It is not through struggle and effort and trying that resistance is released, but instead through distraction and releasing and relaxing.

Our recording holds within it a perfect Vibrational formula for the releasing of the only hindrance to everything you desire. If you will allow it, it will gently and gradually guide you to the allowance of all that you are asking for.

Your life is supposed to feel good to you, and you are meant to satisfy your dreams. There is nothing more satisfying than the deliberate alignment with what you have dreamed.

16

You are doing extremely well.

The Well-Being that you seek is flowing to you.

Relax and enjoy the unfolding; and feel appreciation

for *what-is*, and eagerness for what is coming. . . .

There is great love here for you.

And, as always, we remain—in the Vortex.

You will experience incremental feelings of relief as you gradually allow your resistance to be released, just as you find relief in drinking when you are thirsty, or eating when you are hungry.

The Eternal nature of your Being and the magnificent platform of expansion upon which you stand will hold you in a steady quest or thirst for that expansion, with unending satisfaction stretching out before you.

The perfect contrast of your time-space reality will continue to stimulate your thirst while also holding the promise to fulfill every desire that has been inspired.

Whether you are focused upon contrast in this moment—and so, are in the process of *asking* for more—or whether you are focused on your breathing in this moment and are *allowing* what you have asked for, it is all part of the process, and it is all on your path.

As your question comes into greater clarity, your answer comes into greater clarity as well. As your problem comes into greater focus, your solution comes into greater focus as well. Our recording will make it easier for you to find resonance with the solution. Your repeated listening to the recording will allow any problems to move into the background, and the solutions to move into the foreground.

Over time, your appreciation for the question will become equivalent to your appreciation for the answer, and your appreciation for the problem will become equivalent to your appreciation for the solution. And in your newfound ease with <u>what-is,</u> you will find yourself in the state of allowing what you truly desire. And then, all manner of cooperative components will reveal themselves to you in a delicious co-creative dance of Deliberate Creation.

Meditation:
Financial Abundance

1

We are going to stand for a while
in your physical shoes and speak words
that are of greatest advantage to you.
For we want to help you find the Vibrational stance to allow
financial abundance to flow into your personal experience.

Sometimes, even though you are asking for a specific desire to be fulfilled, you are not actually moving toward the fulfillment of your desire, but instead you are actually moving further from it. And even though you think you are *asking* for what you do want, your request is actually being made from your *awareness of its absence*.

You usually feel discouraged when a great deal of time passes while you "work" on your desire, but the results you are seeking do not materialize. We want to help you to understand that you simply cannot get there from there: *you cannot get to where you want to be when you are keenly aware of its absence.*

Rather than saying, "I want more money," say instead, "I want to *feel* my financial well-being." You see, it is possible to *feel* an increased sense of financial well-being even before the money comes. But when you are focused upon the *desire* for the money, and taking score of the *absence* of the money, you are Vibrationally defeating your own purpose.

Rather than saying, "I want [or need] a new car," say instead, "I like the *feeling* of Well-Being that comes with the driving of a new car"—because you can accomplish that feeling even before you drive the new car; and once the *feeling* is consistently within you, the new car, and many other things that match your feeling of security, will flow to you.

As you allow the Law-based words of our recording to play gently in the background of your mind, your resistance to Well-Being will become less, while your allowing of Well-Being will become more. You have only to remember that, at first, the evidence of your improved state of allowing comes in the form of good-feeling emotions, not in the form of money or new cars. But eventually the money and the new cars will come, too.

2

The Stream of abundance flows generously—
and it is right—and it is time for you to receive your share.
This will not be difficult for you to do,
and it will not take much time,
because you are already well along the way.

It is time for the financial abundance that you have been seeking to materialize into your experience, not because you have paid
a large enough price for it through diligence and hard work, but
because you now understand that it is not diligence and hard work
that brings it—but Vibrational alignment with abundance.

Through the life that you have been living, and the contrast
that you have been sifting through, you have planted and cultivated
many fields of abundance that are now ready for your harvest and

enjoyment. It is not about your earning and deserving, but about your understanding and alignment with your desired Well-Being.

The Stream of abundance is not a quantifiable volume to be fairly proportioned until its limits have been reached, for there is no limit to this abundance or to those who drink from its Stream. The Stream of abundance expands proportionately to satisfy the ever-increasing requests, not only keeping perfect pace with the requests, but expanding because of them.

Because your requests have been in the process of becoming for some time, and because the Stream has expanded to accommodate those requests, your only work now is to come into Vibrational alignment with your requests in order to experience the complete satisfaction of their certain materialization.

The amount of time that will pass between now and the manifestation of your desires is strictly about the time that it takes for you to replace angst with ease.

It is our expectation that—as a result of your daily participation with our recording—your resistance will subside, you will begin to feel better and better, your relationship with the financial abundance that you desire will improve . . . and that this will not be difficult for you to do.

≼ 3 ≽

There is power in the words that you are hearing;
and, in time, your resistance will subside,
and your allowing will begin. As your *resistance*
is replaced with *allowing*—as *doubt* is replaced
with *belief*—your *abundance* will become evident.

Even though we stand in complete awareness of the financial abundance that is queued up and waiting for you, our knowledge of your abundance cannot be instantly transferred to you even when we offer you powerful words that reflect our knowing.

So the Vibrational shift that will take place within you as you listen to our recording will not be because of the power of our words or the truth of our message, but instead, it will be because of *your* Vibrational shift.

From your human perspective, you often believe that you must work hard to overcome obstacles and satisfy shortages and solve the problems that are before you; but often, in that attitude or approach, you work against yourself without realizing it. *Attention to obstacles makes them bigger and more stubborn; attention to shortages makes them bigger and prolongs them—and attention to a problem prevents any immediate resolution or solution.*

As you listen to our recording, giving your attention to your breathing and to the natural rhythm of your body, any problematic Vibrational activation will simply cease to be. And, in the absence of that resistance, your Vibration will naturally begin to rise until it will align with the higher Vibration of the very solutions you have been longing for.

In the absence of longing, in the absence of doubt—in the absence of obstacles and shortages and problems—will be the solutions and abundance that you seek. And the evidence of your Vibrational shift will become obvious in two ways: first, you will feel better; and next, physical evidence of financial improvement will begin flowing to you from a variety of different directions.

≼ 4 ≽

Our words will help you to shift your feeling
about money from worry or concern to eagerness and fun.
When that emotional shift occurs,
immediate financial manifestations will be
the evidence of that shift.

After only a few days of listening to our recording—and relaxing and breathing—your releasing of resistance will be apparent to you in the releasing of tension in your body. You will not only feel more ease, but also you will feel more clarity and more physical invigoration.

As your resistance subsides and you come into fuller alignment, you will begin to feel a fuller resonance with the words that you have been hearing. It is a very satisfying experience when words that you were hearing and understanding in a logical or intellectual way shift to an emotional-resonance sort of understanding.

You may begin to feel physical sensations of thrills or goose bumps rippling through your body to indicate the Vibrational alignment that you have achieved. And when that Vibrational shift occurs, it is like walking from a small, dark room out into the beautiful light of day, where *confusion* is replaced with *clarity,* and *uncertainty* is replaced with *knowing.*

Once that Vibrational shift occurs within you, all manner of evidence will confirm it:

- Good-feeling ideas will flow abundantly to you.

- Things that you have been wondering about will come into greater clarity.

- Things that you have been meaning to do will present themselves to you in an obvious and easy-to-accomplish manner.

- Problems that have seemed stubborn will seem to resolve themselves without your personal involvement.

- And money and opportunities will begin to show up in your experience in surprising and unexpected ways.

◦〈 5 〉◦

If we can convince you
that the path to financial abundance
is simply an emotional path, then, with each
hearing of these words, you will breathe out
more resistance—and your feelings will improve.

It is our desire that you approach this 15-minute daily meditation as a time of refreshing and relaxing, rather than a time of study and learning.

Your awareness of your breathing will be the powerful key to your releasing of resistance and the raising of your Vibration. And then, the words that we are speaking will be heard by you in a new and profound way.

There is a big difference between *hearing* an answer and *understanding* it. There are many people who are outside the Vortex who are hearing words, but it is only those who are inside the Vortex who are truly understanding.

We want you to understand that the true path to the abundance and financial freedom that you seek is not a journey of action but instead an emotional journey.

Your true power comes from the leverage of your alignment, not from your action. And while it is certain that there will be plenty of action involved, it will be good-feeling action that is inspired from your place of alignment from inside your Vortex.

So, the path to certain financial abundance and financial freedom is this:

- *Find 15 minutes every day to give to this process.*

- *Focus your undivided attention, as best you can, upon your breathing.*

- *Enjoy the feeling of breathing. Enjoy the feeling of syncing your breath with the music.*

- *Feel the ease of your breathing.*

- *Feel the benefit of your breathing.*

- *Enjoy the physical sensation of releasing resistance and allowing your entrance into your Vortex.*

⊰ 6 ⊱

Your work is not one of action.
There are no courses to complete.
There are no requirements for you to meet—
just a comfortable and gradual rediscovery of
your natural state of relief, and of ease, and of Well-Being.

These words are offered to you from our place of understanding that your true power does not come from your physical action, but instead from your *Vibrational alignment.* Your true power and leverage comes from alignment with your intentions and desires. It is never realized when Vibrational resistance is present.

Most rarely align with their true power, because it seems illogical to them that there is power in relaxation, in letting go, or in love or joy or bliss. Most people do not understand that their true power lies in releasing resistance—which is the only obstacle to their true power.

Most people do not expect their path to great abundance to be one of ease and of joy. They have been taught that struggle and hardship and sacrifice are requirements that must be met before the reward of great abundance can be realized. Most do not understand that the very struggle they deliberately involve themselves in, in their quest for success and advantage, actually works *against* them.

There are so many things that you have been taught to believe that are counter to the powerful <u>Laws of the Universe</u> that it is difficult for you to <u>think</u> your way out. And that is the reason that we present this path of much less resistance.

We want you to *breathe* rather than *try,* to *relax* rather than offer *effort,* to *smile* rather than *struggle,* to *be* rather than *do.*

For we know that, in your attention to the music, to your breathing, and eventually to our words (as you discover the true resonance of their meaning), you will reclaim your true alignment with the abundance that you seek and deserve.

Your true power is experienced only from inside the Vortex.

You are never deprived when someone else gains,
because abundance expands proportionately to match desires.
When the success of another makes your heart sing,
your resistance is gone and your
own success soars.

Many people believe that there is not enough to go around because they are experiencing the lack of something wanted in their own experience. But the shortage that they are experiencing is not because there is not enough to go around; it is only because they have Vibrationally cut themselves off from the abundant supply.

Many believe that there is a quantifiable financial limit that is spread thin, as more people strive to partake of it, and they often feel jealousy or blame as they condemn others for taking more than their fair share. They also feel guilty when they believe that *they* are taking more than *their* fair share.

We want you to understand that abundance expands proportionately to match desire, and that there is great untapped abundance not yet allowed by the very humans who have created it. When your life experience causes a focused desire within you, the means to fulfill that desire is created at the same time—but you have to be on the Vibrational wavelength with your desire in order to see the path to the fulfillment of it.

A belief in *shortage* or *lack* will prevent your discovery of the path to your own creation, and any feeling of resistance indicates that you are on the wrong Vibrational path. However, in your understanding of the never-ending *abundance* of this Universe, you will feel personal delight whenever you observe anyone's alignment with it, for their achievement can in no way diminish yours, but can only enhance it.

As you focus upon your breathing and the music and words of the recording, you will deactivate your usual resistance to abundance, and you will discover the satisfying feeling of positive expectation and success. And then, the manifestation of that success must come to you. It is Law!

⊰ 8 ⊱

The fastest way to get to an
improved financial condition is to look for pleasing things
that you already have, for in the seeking and finding
of that which is working, more success
will come—and it will come quickly.

Your improved state of emotion will not be limited only to the 15 minutes that you are participating in the guided meditation, but will extend into many of your other waking moments.

And because of your gradual and consistent releasing of resistance, your Vibrational frequency will move to higher and higher set points, or averages.

Because of the improvement in your Vibrational point of attraction, and because of the releasing of resistance and the raising of your

Vibrational frequency, you will have access, on a daily basis, to better-and-better-feeling thoughts.

Now that you have established an improved Vibrational set point, you will be able to see evidence of financial improvement in your day-to-day experience that has not been obvious before.

When you make a decision to look for positive aspects in the experience that is unfolding right now, you will create an expectation that will allow an immediate manifesting of evidence to support that Vibrational shift. In other words, the more you look for positive aspects of your current life, the more positive aspects will step forward to reveal themselves to you.

During your 15-minute meditation process, you will have found a way to feel abundance without the need to see evidence of it. But, over time, you will be able to see what you were not able to see before. And with a bit more time, you will become completely expectant of good things to come into your experience.

The fastest way to bring more wonderful examples of abundance into your personal experience is to take constant notice of the wonderful things that are already there. The abundance that you allow is always a perfect match to your expectation.

While your life will continue to call more abundance
to you, the majority of that work is already done.
And now, with far less effort than you
have been believing, your financial condition
is about to improve.

Without realizing it, you have been sifting through the experience of your life and summoning unspeakable abundant resources to your Vortex, where they remain waiting for your alignment with them. This abundance has been defined and refined by you and cannot be kept from you or taken from you. It remains as your creation, and can be claimed only by you.

Your abundance that is banked in your Vortex of Creation will continue to expand, because your life will continue to call more abundance through you. *If it ever feels to you as if you have come to the end of the resources that you have set aside, it will not be because you have reached the end, but simply because you are depriving yourself of what is there—for there is no ending to the resources of the Vortex. The process of life assures that.*

With every listening to the guided meditation on financial abundance, your resistance will become less, and your allowing will be more, until one day you will read the words that are written upon this page and you will understand, without question, the true worthiness of your Being.

You will stand in complete acceptance of your value, offering no resistance whatsoever to the evidence of your value. You will feel no discomfort as the blessings of abundance and Well-Being shower down around you, indicating your alignment with the worthy Being that you are.

It is not possible for you to achieve Vibrational alignment with the abundance of your Vortex without the manifestational evidence of that abundance showing up. Others around you will undoubtedly see evidence of your abundance, but you will know that what they are seeing is really evidence of your <u>alignment.</u>

❧ 10 ❧

Financial abundance does not
occur in one's life because of hard work
or good luck or favoritism—financial abundance
is simply the Universe's response to consistent
thoughts and feelings of abundance.

There are many people who are approaching life from the flawed premise that if they work hard and struggle long and pay a big enough price, they will then be rewarded with financial well-being. And since they do not realize that in their struggle they are denying themselves alignment with the abundance they seek, when the abundance does not come, they attribute it to *luck* or *favoritism* that is being directed away from them and toward another.

But there is no luck or favoritism. There is only allowing or resisting, allowing or denying, letting in or keeping out the abundance that you deserve.

When you see evidence of shortage and you attribute it to action or intention or power that is outside of you, then your only course of action is to try to win favor from whoever holds the power. But since this power is not being held by someone outside of you, looking for it there will not bring you positive results.

As you gradually train your own thoughts into those of positive expectation, as you align with thoughts of worthiness and Well-Being, as you align with your true power by seeking good-feeling thoughts—you will no longer offer resistance to your own abundance. And when your resistance stops, your abundance will come. A flood of good-feeling ideas and possibilities will flow to you. Interesting and exciting conversations will surround you. People of influence and means will seek you out and find you. Opportunities and propositions will be plentiful. And soon you will stand in knowing amusement that all of this was always there within your reach, but in your resistant state of attraction, you were not yet able to experience it . . . but then, it came—not because of your struggle but because of your ease.

When you are able to accomplish
the *feeling* of abundance before the *evidence*
has shown itself to you, the evidence must come,
and will continue to come as long as you
maintain the feeling of abundance.

It is a rather easy thing to feel good when you are experiencing the manifestation of something that you want. It is easy to be pleased while witnessing only pleasing things. But if you only have the ability to respond to what you are observing, then the only way to consistently feel good would be to control the environment around you so that it contains only what you consider to be good things.

You would either have to control the behavior of all others or you would have to drastically restrict the scope of your own experience. And, of course, that is not possible.

We want you to understand that while feelings do come in response to what you are *observing*, feelings also come in response to what you are *thinking*, and you have the ability to think far beyond what you are observing. And while it is possible to gradually train your thoughts (apart from what you are observing) to increasingly pleasing subjects until your beliefs about things begin to shift, there is a faster way of shifting Vibration, of feeling better, and of shifting your point of attraction to more pleasing experiences:

Our guided-meditations recording is an effective shortcut to improving your point of attraction, because as you successfully align your breathing with the rhythm of the music on the recording, you will be distracted from usual resistant thoughts. And because your resistant thoughts are temporarily deactivated, your Vibration will rise. In the raising of your Vibration, you will come into alignment with the Source within you. Because of that alignment—you will feel better. Because of that alignment—you will be inside your Vortex of Creation. Because you are inside your Vortex of Creation—you will be in alignment with abundance. Because you are in alignment with abundance—it must manifest.

⋖ 12 ⋗

Anytime you are feeling good,
no matter the reason, you are
accomplishing the feeling of abundance;
and in your absence of resistance, everything that
you have asked for is making its way right to you.

When you feel deprived . . .
When you feel taken advantage of . . .
When you feel mistreated . . .
When you feel misunderstood . . .
When you feel poor . . .
. . . the evidence of your belief will show itself to you.

The evidence of *your belief!* Not the evidence of your value, or the evidence of your worthiness. This is not a punishment for your sins, or a withholding of God's love. This is not luck, or favoritism, or injustice or unfairness, or bad karma. _What you are living, all day, every day, is the manifested evidence of your own belief!_

A belief is only a thought you continue to think. A belief is a Vibration that you have practiced often enough that now it is dominant and therefore comes up easily and often. A belief is a Vibrational point of attraction that brings evidence of itself to you.

When you feel happy . . .

When you feel exhilarated . . .

When you feel satisfied . . .

When you feel eager . . .

When you feel excited . . .

When you feel understood . . .

When you feel blessed . . .

When you feel honored . . .

When you feel abundant . . .

. . . the evidence of your belief will show itself to you.

Our daily guided meditation will help you release resistance. The releasing of resistance will give you access to better-feeling thoughts, and the more you access those better-feeling thoughts, the more they will become dominant. The daily meditation will help you shift your beliefs—and your new beliefs will bring new evidence in the form of abundance manifestation.

Each time you focus upon these words, your resistance
becomes smaller, and your allowance becomes greater.
And so, with each passing day, your Vibrational
point of attraction will change until there
will be an obvious tipping point.

The benefits of this daily meditation process will reach beyond the actual 15 minutes that you will be spending every day. It is certain that during meditation you will feel an increase of alignment, but while the mental and physical benefits will be physically felt by you during your meditation, the benefit of your releasing of resistance will follow you into every aspect of your day.

Every current relationship will be transformed, and every activity will be positively affected at all levels of your being . . . and every interaction with every aspect of your life will feel better. The better you feel—the better it gets.

This daily meditation process will help you accomplish an effective releasing of long-standing resistance, and every day, the benefits of that release of resistance will be more evident to you. Every day, the frequency of your desires and the frequency of your beliefs will come into closer Vibrational range. And then, one day, not long after you begin this daily meditation process, the vibration of your formerly resistant beliefs will give way to the power of your desire. That desire has been powerfully pulsing within you, but your learned and practiced resistance has kept it muted or hindered.

With the gradual releasing of resistance, you will feel an actual tipping point—a sort of breaking-loose feeling, a feeling of coming out into the light—and then your manifested world will never be the same. . . . All manner of physical, tangible, seeable, hearable, touchable experiences will begin to manifest; and it will be obvious, to anyone who is watching, that something has shifted for you. It will seem to others that your luck has shifted, but you will know that it is not luck that shifted, but your Vibrational relationship to your own desires.

⊰ 14 ⊱

For a while, the only evidence of your financial progress
will be your improved emotional state of being,
and if you will let that be enough—taking
no score of financial progress—the
financial improvement will show up.

Prior to the Vibrational tipping point, which is accompanied by obvious tangible physical improvements, there has been other Vibrational progress being made. And that Vibrational progress can be felt through your improved emotional state, even though tangible evidence is not yet discernible.

If you are willing to let your improved emotional state be the evidence of your progress, then the progress will continue; you will continue to feel even better, and the tipping point will come where physical evidence can be seen.

But if you look too soon for the evidence, and you do not yet find it, you will lose Vibrational ground.

The need to see the immediate evidence of progress is the most significant hindrance to most people. When you attempt to take score of your progress too soon, you move further from the results you seek.

There is no desire that you hold that is for any other reason than you believe you would feel better in the having of it. Whether it is a material object, a pile of money, a relationship, a physical state of being—every desire is wanted because you want to feel better.

When you discover the power of feeling better first, by the deliberate focusing of your mind away from problems, struggles, irritants, and any other manner of unwanted things—and focus your mind upon the simplicity of your own breathing—you will have found the key to the power of allowing.

Evidence of everything you desire is making its way to you, and the only thing that is holding it back is your offering of a consistent Vibration that disallows it. When you discover the simple art of no longer offering that unnecessary and uncomfortable resistance, you will let in everything that you have been asking for.

≼ 15 ≽

We are so pleased to have this opportunity to express
to you our appreciation for all that you are.
We want to let you know that it is
our absolute promise to you that
the abundance you seek is coming.

We have long enjoyed witnessing the expanding Universe and the important part that you play in that expansion as your life causes you to launch continuing desires. But we are particularly exhilarated as we anticipate your conscious realization of your true creative power.

There is nothing more delicious than to have *conscious* awareness of a personal desire, *conscious* recognition of resistance that is preventing or slowing the manifestation, *conscious* releasing of that resistance, and then *conscious* recognition of the manifestation. That is Deliberate (Conscious) Creation at its best!

There is no end to life experience, for you are an Eternal Being with never-ending opportunities for joyous expansion.

With each new desire that is launched and then allowed to manifest—you will discover yet another platform from which to launch more desire. This process of creation is not about getting the creation finished and finding an end to needed manifestations. It is about the joyous process of *expansion.* And in the very moment that your intention shifts to a determination to "feel good" rather than a determination of "manifest something," not only will you become a consistently happy person, but all things wanted will flow easily to you.

It seems a paradox to some—in the beginning—while it is not paradoxical at all: "I want these things because I would feel better in the having of them, but my awareness of their absence prevents me from having them. But if I can find a way of feeling better even without having them, then they can be mine."

A powerful Universal truth is simply this: you cannot attract the presence of something wanted when predominantly aware of its absence.

You are doing extremely well.
Abundance is flowing to you.
Relax; enjoy the unfolding; and feel appreciation for
what-is, and eagerness for what is coming. . . .
There is great love here for you.

And, as always, we remain—in the Vortex.

We appreciate your awareness that you are a Vibrational Being.
We appreciate your awareness of the importance of your emotions.
We appreciate your willingness to focus daily upon your breathing.
We appreciate the Vibrational shifts that are already occurring within you.

We appreciate your consistent releasing of resistance.

We appreciate the continual opening of new doors, allowing your further discovery of *who-you-are.*

We are eager about the consistent ease that is before you.

We are eager about your new desires still to be launched.

We are eager for your inevitable rendezvous with good-feeling ideas and experiences.

We are eager for your realization of the details of your manifested world.

We are eager for your realization of the unlimited abundance that surrounds you.

We are eager for your realization of your desires.

We are eager to watch the details of your Deliberate Creation make their way into your experience.

We are eager for your feeling of fulfillment that is certain.

We are eager for the tipping point that surely will come that will allow you to see yourself as we know you to be: deserving of all manner of abundance, worthy of all good things, satisfied with <u>what-is</u>—*and eager for more.*

There is great love here for you!

Meditation:
Physical Well-Being

1

It is nice to have an opportunity to visit with you
for the purpose of tuning to your natural rhythm of Well-Being.
Your intelligent body is comprised of trillions of cells,
and they are seeking and finding alignment
and balance at all times.

While it is obvious that a good-feeling body makes for a more pleasant physical experience, we want you to understand that finding pleasant things to focus upon also makes for a good-feeling body.

However, most humans are approaching the subject of their physical well-being in a backward manner. Most people who are experiencing physical ailments let their physical condition dictate their mental attitude. In other words, their emotions are responsive to their physical condition. When they are in pain, they offer emotions of frustration, worry, anger, or fear. They want the condition to improve so that their emotional state can improve.

Any illness, or departure from physical well-being, begins at a cellular level—but the overwhelming propensity of your cells is that of thriving. All day, every day, your cells are reclaiming balance at such refined and subtle levels that most people are completely unaware of the power and intelligence of their cellular bodies.

This continual realigning and rebalancing process hinges on cellular communication: communication from one cell to another, and Vibrational communication between the physical and Non-Physical aspects of those cells. And when you are feeling negative emotion, you are in the state of hindering that cellular communication.

While your physical body is extremely resilient—and has evolved to maintain significant balance even while communication is hindered—the evidence of chronic worry or anger or overwhelment does show up in the form of diminished physical well-being.

Focusing upon good-feeling objects of attention is the most effective way of providing the optimum environment for allowing unhindered cellular communication and the ultimate thriving of your physical body.

2

There is no greater advantage that you could
offer to your body than this gentle releasing of resistance,
right now—for your natural state is one of absolute Well-Being,
and in the absence of resistance,
your physical body must thrive.

Relief always feels good, and there are many things of an action nature that can give you a feeling of relief: When you are thirsty, your body feels the relief of something refreshing to drink. When you are hungry, it is a relief to eat something. When you are tired, it is a relief to rest. But if you wait until your body is completely dehydrated before you drink something or completely emaciated before you eat something, your body can get far out of balance. *While it is possible to eventually bring your body back to a state of* well-being—*it is much easier to maintain a healthy physical balance than to recover it after losing it.*

Most people never put themselves into the dramatic situation where they are without water or food to the point of doing damage to their physical bodies; however, it is not uncommon for people to deprive their bodies of something equally important: alignment with Source Energy.

Often people develop patterns of thought that hold them steadily in a state of negative emotion. And even though they grow accustomed to the feelings of overwhelment, anger, worry, blame, guilt, and so forth, the chronic negative emotions indicate strong patterns of resistance that are hindering to natural Well-Being.

In the same way that it is a good idea to drink when you feel the indication of thirst—and therefore maintain your Well-Being long before dehydration is experienced—it is equally important to change the thought and release resistance at the first indication of negative emotion. For while it is certainly possible to withstand negative emotion for long periods of time, it is not the optimal experience for the cells of your physical body.

When you learn to release resistance in the early, subtle stages, your physical body must thrive. Thriving is what is natural to you.

By deliberately focusing upon good-feeling thoughts,
you allow your physical cells to return to their natural balance.
Breathing deeply is the key, softly hearing
our words and allowing gentle alignment
with the Energy of your Source. . . .

Positive emotion is your indication that you are approaching the subject of your thought in the same way that the Source within you is. In other words, the feeling of love that you are feeling for someone matches the way Source feels about him or her.

Negative emotion is your indication that you are approaching the subject of your thought in the opposite way than the Source within you is. For example, the feeling of hatred or anger that you are feeling for someone does not match the way Source feels about him or her.

The better you feel, emotionally, the more you are allowing your alignment with Source. The worse you feel, the more you are resisting Source. When no resistance is being offered by you, your natural state of alignment resumes—and so does the alignment between your cells and their Source.

As you listen to the music in our recording and gently focus with the intention of syncing your breathing to the rhythm of the music, you will release all resistance; and in the absence of any resistant Vibration, your Vibration naturally will rise.

During your first days or weeks of your daily participation with the recording, your cellular relief will occur primarily during the 15 minutes that you are listening and relaxing and breathing. But eventually—because of your daily focusing upon your breathing and releasing of resistance—the *Law of Attraction* will sync you up with better-and-better-feeling thoughts.

The more good-feeling thoughts you focus upon, the more you allow the cells of your body to thrive. You will notice a marked improvement in clarity, agility, stamina, and vigor, for you are literally breathing your way to Well-Being, until chronic feelings of appreciation, love, eagerness, and joy will confirm that you have released all resistance and are now allowing Well-Being.

≼ 4 ≽

The cells of your body are guided
by Source; and they have the ability to find
their balance, no matter what, every time.
And so, you will not only find recovery from unwanted conditions,
but a steady maintaining of Well-Being will ensue.

Your sophisticated physical body exists because of the intelligence of your cells. And the intelligence of your cells exists because of their Connection to Source Energy.

Doctors, of course, are aware when your physical body is no longer the receiver of Source Energy, and so they pronounce you "DEAD." But there is much, much more for them to come to understand about the connection between your cellular physical body and the Vibrational Energy of Source.

When doctors and scientists try to find cures for diseases without taking into consideration the Vibrational relationship between the physical Being and Source Energy, they are looking for cures in all the wrong places. If the resistance that disallowed the Well-Being to begin with is not released, it will show up in the form of another and another disease. *Dis-ease is the disallowing of ease. Dis-ease is the disallowance of Well-Being, which is always indicated, pre-disease, in the form of chronic negative emotion.*

Your cells, because of their connection to the intelligence of Source Energy, know exactly what to do in order to become the incredible variety of functioning cells in your magnificent physical body. And in the absence of the hindrance that is caused by your resistant negative thought, that communication stays open to clear, up-to-the-moment interaction, keeping your physical body at peak and perfect performance.

In the absence of negative emotion—and therefore the allowance of complete alignment and communication with Source Energy—your physical body can reclaim its balance and recover from any imbalance. And once balance has resumed, it is easy to maintain with consistently good-feeling thoughts.

❖ 5 ❖

As you listen and breathe—and release and relax—
the maintaining of a good-feeling body will come easily.
Even unwanted conditions that have been within you
for a while will gradually diminish
until they no longer exist.

Through this daily process of focusing upon your breathing, you will progressively breathe your resistance away, causing a gradual shift in your Vibrational point of attraction. And then, you will begin to feel a strong resonance with the words that we have been speaking to you. When that occurs, the Vibration of your physical body and that of the Source within you will be at the same Vibrational frequency; and when that occurs, your physical body will benefit. *Unwanted conditions will fall away, one by one. With no big fanfare and no celebration of dramatic healing, your physical body will gradually return to its natural state of well-being.*

In the same way that a complete understanding of electricity is unnecessary in order to flip the switch and receive the benefit of it, you do not need to understand the complex inner workings of your physical body. You only need to understand the simple process by which you allow your intelligent cells to do their work.

We like to say to you that if you were no longer doing that thing you do—which causes resistance—your Vibration would rise. But here is the larger picture: When you focus upon your breathing (and the recording really requires focus in order to get into rhythm), you cannot be focused upon resistance-causing thoughts at the same time. As you release those resistance-causing thoughts, your Vibration rises. As your Vibration rises, you begin to hear and understand the words we are speaking.

As you find and practice resonance with the Vibration of the Source within you, communication between the cells of your body flourishes, as does your entire physical body. And it all begins with the simple focusing upon your breathing to "flip the switch" of absolute physical well-being.

❖ 6 ❖

By releasing resistance
a little more every day, you will feel the power
that creates worlds flowing through you . . .
just breathing and listening, not to make something happen,
but for the pleasure and comfort of alignment.

Your releasing of resistance will be a gradual, progressive experience, with each day of improved Vibration building upon the day before.

Because it is gradual, you may go for a few days without any noticeable difference in your point of attraction and the experiences you are having; but soon, there will be a tipping point, and you will then notice substantial changes in your life experience.

Not only will you notice an improvement in the way you feel, with a substantial lifting of your daily mood, but your interactions with your life in general will show you that your point of attraction has shifted. Every interaction with friends, family, and strangers will reflect your Vibrational shift and your releasing of resistance.

This wonderful improvement in the way your life feels and works will happen because you are not trying to fix anything. In fact, you are doing the opposite of <u>trying</u>—you are <u>allowing.</u> Because of your pure and simple intention of focusing upon your breathing, gently syncing with the music, and softly listening to the words we are offering—all for the pleasure and comfort of the moment of alignment—your resistance will fall away and your Vibration will rise.

Without setting goals, without checking off lists of things to be accomplished, the Universe will demonstrate to you that you are becoming a master of allowing those things that you have been asking for to flow easily to you.

Literally, every single day of this process will yield you a higher balance of Vibration, which means, every day, your point of attraction will improve. Every day, you will feel substantially better, and you will notice marked improvements in the quality of your attraction on all subjects.

Your physical body will respond very quickly
to the absence of resistance that you are feeling
while you breathe, for there is no physical body,
no matter what the condition, that cannot return
to its natural state of well-being.

Your focused attention to your breathing is beneficial in two important ways:

1. Your attention to your breathing will distract your attention from unwanted thoughts, thereby causing you to release resistance. And in the absence of resistance, your cells are now communicating in an optimum fashion.

2. Because you are breathing more deeply than usual during a time of no resistance, the oxygenation of your cells will

> improve dramatically. And so, your body will feel more
> alive because, at a cellular level, it *is* more alive.

Our daily process is a way in which you are providing the best possible environment for the intelligent cells of your body to do their work of bringing your body into optimal balance.

In your world today there are countless action remedies, medicines, surgeries, and exercises offered—but there are not enough actions in the world to compensate for Vibrational resistance.

This daily meditation will provide a basis, or nucleus, for physical improvement; and it will also enhance any other treatments and remedies that you may already be involved in.

Since every disease or unwanted condition exists because Well-Being is being disallowed, then, in the absence of that disallowance, Well-Being will return.

It is a common thing for people to begin to lean in the direction of recovery, only to stop and take score too soon. And when they still find unwanted symptoms or conditions, they then offer resistant thought and lose the improved ground they have gained. With consistent releasing of resistance, all unwanted conditions will subside, returning you to your natural state of Well-Being.

⊰ 8 ⊱

These words you are hearing are not about your body—
but about your allowing and alignment of Source.
Your body is a reflection of the balance
of your thought, and this release of resistance
will produce positive change.

By focusing simply upon your Vibrational relationship with the Energy of your Source, you will be distracted from any unwanted conditions of your physical body. And as you withdraw your attention from those unwanted conditions, they will cease to exist.

Resistant thought regarding any number of things causes a pinching off of Well-Being, which then allows the unwanted condition to appear. And then, attention to the unwanted condition continues the perpetuation of it.

A withdrawal of attention from the unwanted condition is necessary in order to release it from your experience, but it is also necessary to cease the resistant thought that pinched off the Well-Being to begin with. Our meditation process helps accomplish both of those things, and it lays the basis of a new-and-improved outlook on life. . . . You will find it easier to find increasingly better things to think about. It will be easier to see the positive aspects in situations and people. You will find compliments flowing from you, and you will feel appreciation for more things.

The less resistant thoughts you think, the better you will feel; and the better you feel, the less resistant thoughts you will think. And because of all of that, your point of attraction will improve, causing improved manifestation of relationships and finances, as well as bodily conditions.

Your physical body is truly a reflection of the thoughts you think, but not only of the thoughts you think about your physical body. And so, understanding the Vibrational basis that supports your physical body is important to your maintaining of a healthy physical body. A regimen of physical actions is not enough. Your body is a pure reflection of the balance of the thoughts that you think.

Beginning with the cells of your physical body,
physical improvement will sweep through you at every level.
You are a Vibrational Being with Non-Physical roots,
and your body is an extension of
that Non-Physical Source.

There is a powerful leverage available to you that most people are unaware of, and a daily utilization of our meditation process will give you access to it whether you are consciously aware of it or not. And then, because of your personal experience, enhanced and confirmed by the words you are reading here, you will have full conscious awareness of this leverage.

When you understand that you are a Vibrational Being, first and foremost—and that your dominant intention becomes that of tuning your Vibrational frequency to that of the Source within you—you will provide the perfect basis for the cells of your physical body to thrive. But if you are approaching your physical body from the usual physical standpoint, noticing symptoms and analyzing your physical condition, you will emit Vibrational resistance that hinders your well-being. In other words, your Vibrational response to your current condition makes it difficult to overcome any unwanted physical condition.

When you are able to find 15 minutes in every day to relax and tune to the frequency of your Source, during that time of meditation, all resistance and hindrance will cease, allowing the cells of your body the opportunity to return to their natural state of Well-Being. And your improved Vibrational state will then begin to spread through larger segments of your day.

The simple process of breathing, and releasing resistance, allows your Vibrational alignment with your Source, which then allows a definite shift in the Vibration of your cells and a renewal of cellular well-being.

At the root of your physical condition is the condition of your cells. At the root of the physical condition of your cells is a Vibrational pattern. At the root of that Vibrational pattern is alignment with the Well-Being of the Source within you.

❧ 10 ❧

We offer these words so—as you listen
and breathe—you will tune to your
frequency of natural Well-Being.
When you take the time to find Vibrational balance,
your physical well-being will be easy to maintain.

Most people, while experiencing something unwanted, try hard to improve their situation, not realizing that their dominant awareness of the unwanted condition or situation prevents them from finding the improvement that they desire. It is easy to understand why so many people feel so much discouragement about so many things. They simply cannot get there, from there.

Our daily meditation process will help you to first reach a different kind of goal—the goal of emotional relief and Vibrational improvement.

But, even though this is something that you can easily accomplish (even in your first days of meditation), do not underestimate its power.

Because of the Vibrational balance that you will discover, many things that you have been struggling to accomplish or maintain will fall easily into place for you. It will feel to you as if an uncomfortable edginess has lifted, and everyone and everything around you will begin to cooperate with your intentions. And, in a short time, your awareness of your current circumstances, which had been working <u>against</u> you, will begin to work <u>for</u> you, because you will be observing wanted conditions, which will perpetuate more wanted conditions, and so on.

Many people will be amazed at the ease with which they are able to maintain a healthy, good-feeling physical body once they find their Vibrational balance. And it is important to understand that you are never very far from being able to do that. It is just a matter of understanding what is really at the basis of your natural Well-Being, and then doing things that allow that.

It seems counterintuitive to many people that "trying less hard" actually accomplishes more. But when you factor in the powerful flow of Well-Being, and you discover how to tap into that flow, then it all begins to make perfect sense to you.

From your place of alignment, beneficial behavior
will be inspired, and wonderful things will unfold with great ease.
And the more ease you feel, the less resistance
you hold, and the more the cells of
your body can find their balance.

When you are not in Vibrational alignment with your Source, you
are still able to use your willpower to motivate yourself into action,
but there is nothing very pleasant about that kind of behavior; and, in
the larger scheme of things, it is also relatively unproductive.

It is our knowing that once you discover the leverage of Energy
that the Vortex provides—and the ease and flow of aligning with
this Energy that creates worlds—you will never want to return to the
struggle and hard work of being out of the Vortex again. There is a

big difference between *allowing* your natural Well-Being and *trying* to make it happen.

As you settle into the rhythm of consistent alignment with the Energy of your Source, you will feel physically energized and enthusiastic about life. You will find yourself wanting to be more active, not because you need to in order to accomplish things, but because you want to. Any former feelings of overwhelment and struggle will be replaced with new feelings of eagerness and passion. And rather than wanting to retreat and rest, you will want to get out into the world and discover.

Day by day, as your resistance lifts, you will uncover the passion for life that you were born with. And at the same time that your spirits are lifting and your physical stamina is improving—the cells of your body will be thriving as well.

Your new good-feeling attitude is not only an *indication* of the improvement in your physical body—it is the *reason* for it. The happier you feel, the less hindrance you are to your cellular body.

Most people have it backward. They want to feel good in their body so that they can be happy. But the secret is to be happy first—no matter the condition of your body—and then physical well-being must follow.

◦⟨ 12 ⟩◦

This process of *breathing* and *allowing*
makes it possible to get from wherever you are to
wherever you desire, for as you breathe and release resistance,
you tune your Vibrational frequency to that of your
Source and to personal thriving.

When you are surrounded by pleasing things, you can easily perpetuate your positive attitude or good mood simply by observing your
good-feeling surroundings. It is easier to have a high-flying, happy
moment in a physical body that feels good. But the necessity for having pleasing surroundings or conditions in order to feel good is an
unsustainable situation.

*It does feel good to observe something pleasing, but it is not a good idea
to need something pleasing to observe in order to feel good. If your happiness*

is dependent on seeing only pleasing situations, then you eventually become one of many who are futilely attempting to control the conditions that surround them. They never succeed, and they do not sustain long-term happiness. In fact, they are rarely truly happy.

Many people are approaching life exactly backward: control conditions . . . so that they can observe pleasing things . . . so that they can feel good. . . . This daily meditation process will help you to get into the rhythm and flow of the *Laws* that govern the Vibrational Universe in which you live: care about how you feel . . . so that you can guide your thoughts to align with the Vibrational frequencies of Well-Being . . . so that you can rendezvous with pleasing things . . . so that you can feel good. *Feel good for the sake of feeling good, and everything else will take care of itself.*

This process will teach you (since words actually do not teach) that the actual process of creating is really about no longer doing the things that are preventing your Well-Being. And as you release those resistant thoughts and habits of thoughts (beliefs) one by one, your Vibration will rise until it matches the frequency of perfect physical well-being.

13

It is natural for you to feel good
and for you to be well and for you to
experience perfect bodily conditions.
And as you are becoming a Vibrational Match to Well-Being,
your body will show you the evidence of that.

Most human adults have no recent memory of how very good their physical bodies can feel, for they have been depriving themselves of their natural vitality and alignment for quite a long time.

Unwanted diseases or conditions do not suddenly leap into your body or experience, but come about gradually, over time, as a result of your steady deprivation of Energy.

In other words, if every day you are worried about something, or angry about something, you are depriving yourself of the alignment with Source that keeps your physical body in balance and feeling good. And if you are not responding to your negative emotions as they occur and are making an effort to refocus your thoughts to improve your emotional state of being, but are instead doing as most people do—learning to "live with" the negative emotion, accepting it as "normal life in the modern world"—then eventually there will be a Vibrational tipping point, and the unwanted physical symptom will appear.

Through our daily meditation process, you will begin to remember that you are supposed to feel good. Your *natural* range of emotions is one of *hope* and *interest* and *eagerness* and *passion,* and *love* and *appreciation* and *joy;* and this process will help you to consciously retune yourself to your *natural* frequencies, which will therefore cause any unpleasant and unwanted emotions to be much more evident whenever they occur.

So instead of accepting negative emotion rising within you as just a normal part of life, you will understand what it really is: clear, obvious, in-the-moment guidance that requires a deliberate response from you—the response of choosing a better-feeling thought. While a good-feeling body is conducive to good-feeling thoughts, we want you to remember that your good-feeling thoughts will allow your natural good-feeling body.

14

As you listen and breathe,
with every day that passes your alignment with Well-Being
will become stronger; and as you acknowledge these words
in an atmosphere of no resistance, you will
fuel clarity and vitality and Well-Being.

In the same way that endurance of negative emotions was a gradual process that eventually resulted in a tipping point that brought about noticeable evidence of resistance in the form of an unwanted physical condition—your process of releasing this resistance will be gradual as well. *Our daily meditation process will help you to release resistance, a little more every day, until you will experience a Vibrational tipping point back into alignment with Source Energy.*

Suddenly it will feel as if a veil has been lifted, allowing a clear view of things that were not apparent to you before. You'll feel *clarity* and *sureness* and *confidence* and *knowing,* instead of any awkward *confusion* and *uncertainty* that had been there. And soon after you are aware of this profound emotional shift, improved manifestations of all manner will become apparent to you.

Once there, you may find yourself wondering why you were willing to tolerate your self-inflicted separation from Well-Being for so long, but we want you to gently remind yourself of this very important thing: *Until your Vibration shifted, you did not have access to those improved thoughts, to those improved feelings, or to those improved conditions.* <u>*Everything is about Vibration!*</u>

So even as more conditions of your physical life improve and you find more pleasing manifestations to focus upon, it is our powerful encouragement that you continue this daily process of quieting your mind and focusing upon your breathing to allow the continual retuning of your frequencies to the Well-Being of your Source. So then, as you are romping through life and coming across situations that previously contributed to the gradual muting of Well-Being, you'll be adjusting your Vibration on a daily basis, and maintaining your alignment with the Energy of your Source—and with the Energy of thriving.

⊰ 15 ⊱

Your body responds primarily to the content of your thoughts;
and right here, right now, your body is benefiting.
Your life is supposed to feel good to you,
and you are meant to feel happiness in your life—
and you are meant to satisfy your dreams.

What you think (and how you feel because of your thoughts) and what manifests in your experience always match. You get what you think about, whether it is something wanted or unwanted, and that is especially true in regards to your physical body.

Your physical body is the truest reflection of the beliefs that you hold of anything in your experience. It is helpful to understand that a belief is only a thought that you continue to think—and since you do have control of the thoughts you think, you do have the ability to deliberately project thoughts that have a beneficial effect on your physical body.

The more you practice good-feeling thoughts, the more you will allow unhindered cellular communication, and the more your physical body will thrive.

The process of focusing more on the positive aspects of the thoughts you think is something that requires some time and some practice, but there is a way that you can offer powerful benefit to your body right now, even before you have succeeded at training your thoughts into higher frequencies. To train your thoughts to higher frequencies, you have only to release the resistant thoughts that introduce the resistance. In the absence of those resistant thoughts, your Vibration naturally rises.

As you focus upon the guiding rhythm of the meditation music and successfully sync your breaths in and out with our recording, it is certain that you will deactivate any and all resistant thoughts, at least for the time you are participating with this recording. The simple process of focusing your resistance away will return you to the life of happiness and fulfilled dreams that you came here to live. Your life is supposed to feel good to you.

☙ 16 ☙

You are doing extremely well. Physical well-being
is flowing to you. Relax and enjoy the unfolding.
Feel appreciation for *what-is*, and eagerness for what is coming. . . .
There is great love here for you.

And, as always, we remain—in the Vortex.

Because you are deliberately participating in our book and in our recording, we can unequivocally proclaim to you that your success at raising your Vibration is certain. In other words, it is not possible for you to follow these simple guidelines and not release resistance. And the releasing of resistance always means that your Vibration will naturally rise until alignment with your Source Energy is certain. And when that happens, you will be in the state of allowing the essence of all things that you have been desiring to flow into your experience.

Relax and enjoy the feeling of alignment; and take no score, at all, of physical results. Relax and enjoy the gradual raising of your Vibration, and feel proud of yourself for your deliberate involvement in your own Well-Being.

If we have convinced you that you are doing everything that is required to accomplish everything that you desire by focusing into our recording and allowing your Vibrational frequencies to find their natural rhythm, then certain success will be yours.

We have the benefit of standing in the Vibrational frequency of your Vortex, taking delight in the power of all that is here, knowing *who-you-really-are,* and understanding the power of this process; and we feel eager delight in your conscious discovery of the same.

For a little while, do not try to see into your future, and spend no time analyzing the details of what now is. But, instead, float freely on the sounds of our recording and discover the art of allowing your perfect merging with your Source.

We will stand firm in our knowledge of your promise of Well-Being, ever eager to greet you as you reclaim your natural place with us—inside the Vortex. There is great love here for you.

Meditation:
Relationships

It is nice to have this opportunity
to visit about relationships.
There is no subject of greater significance
to you than relationships, for without others,
you could not be you.

Your relationships with the others with whom you share your planet are valuable to you in several ways. It is obvious to most that your diversity of talents and interests creates an overall environment of balance. But you are helpful to one another in other significant ways as well.

Every person with whom you interact is a part of the person you are becoming. Not a single interaction with a single person is left out of the process of your becoming.

Your interaction with others helps you to define your own personal preferences, and even if you are not speaking those preferences out loud, you are projecting them Vibrationally, and they become the foundation of your very expansion.

Many people assume that only pleasing relationships have value, but that is not the case. Your awareness of an unwanted situation evokes from you a clear Vibrational request for something different. And so, even those uncomfortable interactions with others form the Vibrational basis of your expansion.

People often believe that the value of interacting with others is mostly about combining talents and actions in order to accomplish the things that need to be done in a society, but your interaction with one another is much more important than that. You are helping one another define the attributes of your individual and collective expansion. In other words, even the briefest of encounters with another person is actually contributing to your expansion as an Eternal Being.

It is our desire to help you to return to your natural appreciation of the others with whom you are sharing your planet so that you can fully enjoy every encounter with others, no matter how brief, or regardless of whether you agree with them or not.

❈ 2 ❧

The others with whom you share your planet are of
tremendous value to you even when you want different things;
and your Earth environment is large enough
to accommodate all of the variety of
interests, beliefs, and desires.

The more choices that are available to you, the richer your life becomes. In other words, a food buffet with a vast variety of choices holds a greater potential of satisfying you than a limited buffet. Every aspect of your life is enriched when there is variety from which to choose—and your variety of choices has never been greater.

We are not only speaking about the variety of choices that you have regarding lifestyles, but also choices regarding behaviors, emotional responses, personality characteristics, attitudes, moods, reactions to situations. . . . You are surrounded by varieties and options from which you are creating the expanded version of you.

There are many situations, attitudes, lifestyles—even food choices—that you do not want to participate with. Through the living of your life, you have identified many wanted and unwanted aspects, and it is important to remember than none of those unwanted things can jump into your experience, because there is no assertiveness in your attraction-based Universe.

The choices that others make cannot negatively impact your experience unless you include them in your experience through your attention to them. Things come to you only through your Vibrational invitation—and they remain only by your continuing attention to them.

Your Universe is based upon freedom. Freedom for everyone to choose what they give their attention to, and therefore what they choose to experience. And your interaction with one another provides a contrasting basis that assures continual expansion.

When others achieve Vibrational alignment with something they desire, they in no way deprive you of your desires. If your time-space reality has inspired a desire within you, it is certain that your desire can be fulfilled, for your Earth environment has the potential of satisfying the essence of all desires.

❧ 3 ❧

Your differences are of great advantage
in the stimulation of new ideas,
and are important to your expansion.
You came here eagerly anticipating the expansion
that would be born from your interaction with others.

It is easy to understand the concept of *the more variety there is to choose from, the more choices you would have,* but there is an even larger benefit that is born from the contrasting differences that surround you: as the details of *unwanted* things come into focus for you in your physical dimension, equivalent *wanted* things come into focus in the Non-Physical dimension.

Whenever you know emphatically that you *do not want* something, you project a frequency that holds precise information about what you *do want* into your Vortex of Creation. And your *Inner Being,* the Source within you, holds steady to that new-and-improved Vibration. . . . *As a problem is taking shape in your awareness, an equivalent solution is taking shape at the same time; and as questions occur, the equivalent answers are born.*

From your Non-Physical vantage point, before your birth into this physical body, you understood this wonderful process of Eternal expansion, and you came into your physical body with tremendous eagerness. You saw the variety of your planet—and especially the contrasting points of view of the human population—as the perfect basis not only for expansion, but for joyous expansion. You knew that every problem would bring a solution and that every question would bring an answer, and you were thrilled about your part in the creation of those solutions and answers.

Before your birth, you understood the value of contrast, and you believed in your ability to focus in the direction of solutions; but, most important, you felt no aversion to problems, because you knew that they are all part of the process of Eternal expansion. You relished the idea of joyful exploration, personal choosing, and deliberate focus. Co-creating at its best!

≺ 4 ≻

When you understand the value of differing opinions,
you will reap immediate value from every relationship;
and since you cannot make others change to please you,
appreciating them where they are
will give you ease.

The more perspectives that enter the mix, the greater potential for wonderful creations. Even when you feel strong opposition to the opinions or perspectives of others, your interaction with them provides the basis for expansion and solutions and answers that you would not have access to without their seemingly problematic positions.

We encourage you to make peace with everyone who opposes you and with everyone whom you oppose, not only because you cannot insist on their yielding to your perspective but because their opposing perspective is of tremendous benefit to you.

You see, because of your exposure to what you perceive as their *wrong* or *bad* or *unwanted* behavior or perspective—you have given birth to an improved situation. And just as they helped the *problem* side of the equation to come into focus, they helped the *solution* side of the equation to come into focus, also; and that solution waits for you in your Vortex of Creation.

Through our daily meditation process, you will come into alignment with those solutions and creations that are in your Vortex, and from inside your Vortex, you will feel appreciation for everyone who contributed to its becoming. Deciding in advance to appreciate them—even before you are in your Vortex and even before the solutions have shown themselves to you—will shorten the process and bring you faster to the solutions you seek. And, even more important, your life will feel good to you every step along the way.

When you make peace with those who differ in desire and belief and behavior from your ideas of what is appropriate, you do not perpetuate what you consider to be wrong. Instead, you align with the solution side of the equation that has been waiting for you in your Vortex of Creation.

Sometimes it seems like others have
the power to negatively affect your experience,
but that is never true; only your response to them
has the power to pinch you off from the naturally
good-feeling person you are. . . .

It always feels good to notice the positive aspects of another, because in doing so, you remain in complete alignment with the Broader Perspective of the Source within you. And since the positive behavior of others does feel good, it is logical that you would enjoy giving your attention to that.

But if you become reliant on the behavior of others to keep you feeling good, then when you observe unwanted behavior, it is logical that you would not feel good. And the worst part of that is, you then believe that your feeling good is dependent upon their behavior, over which you have no control. And so, a belief that the behavior of others must be controlled—so that your observation of that good behavior will make you feel good—leaves you feeling vulnerable to their behavior.

We would like to help you to understand that neither the good feeling you find when you observe wanted behavior, nor the bad feeling you find when you observe unwanted behavior, is actually the reason that you feel good or bad. The way you feel is only ever about your alignment, or misalignment, with the Source within you. *It is only your relationship with the Source within you (with your own Inner Being) that is the reason for the emotions that you feel.*

While it is nice to find things in your physical environment that enhance your good-feeling alignment with your *Inner Being,* your understanding of why you feel good will make it possible for you to feel good regardless of the behavior of others.

Understanding that the way you feel is really about your Vibrational relationship with your Inner Being—with the Source within you, with the expanded version of you who resides inside your Vortex—gives you complete empowerment and absolute freedom.

✤ 6 ✤

Sometimes others believe that their
happiness depends upon your response to them,
but that is never true; and if you encourage them
to believe that—and stand on your head to please them—
you don't help them, or you.

When others are pleased by your behavior, it often feels very good to you. It is always nice to see others when they are feeling good, and it feels good to know that you had something to do with their feeling good. But if any of them come to rely on your behavior for their good feeling—then both you and they are at a great disadvantage.

If you make your relationship with your <u>Inner Being</u> your top priority, and you deliberately choose thoughts that allow your alignment, you will consistently offer the greatest advantage to the others with whom you *interact. <u>Only when you are aligned with your Source do you have anything to offer another.</u>*

If your behavior is influenced by your desire to keep another person happy, you will lose your Connection to your Source. And it is not possible for you to be happy unless you are in alignment with your Source. Without that alignment, you have nothing to offer another.

Our daily meditation process will help you to consistently release resistance and to come into alignment with the power and clarity and love that is really <u>who-you-are</u>—and then anyone who you hold as your object of attention will benefit.

Others will notice the consistent happiness that you are experiencing, and they can benefit from the power of your example. As you let them know that your happiness is dependent only upon your own ability to focus yourself into alignment with *who-you-really-are,* you can assist them in discovering the same freedom for themselves.

Rather than attempting the impossible task of trying to behave in ways that please others, show them the ease of finding your consistent alignment. . . . <u>You</u> will always find happiness inside <u>your</u> Vortex. And the happiness that <u>they</u> are seeking is inside <u>their</u> Vortex.

⋠ 7 ⋟

When you expect another to succeed without the benefit
of your help—you see them as their Source sees them.
When you believe another needs your help,
and you attempt to shore up their weakness
with your strength—you help them not.

When you are in your Vortex and in alignment with your
Broader Perspective, and are focused upon other humans, your
attention to them is helpful. Whenever you are aligned with the
powerful Energy of your Source, anything you focus upon receives
the benefit of your gaze.

*When you are in your Vortex, and in alignment with your <u>Inner
Being</u>, you are then tuned to seeing only success in the other humans
you are observing. Whenever you are aware of the problems of others, it*

always means that you are not in your Vortex and you are not in alignment with the way the Source within you is viewing them.

When you are feeling the discomfort from seeing other people in a lackful or needy situation, and you decide to help them from your place of discomfort, no lasting value ever occurs, for two important reasons: first, you are not in alignment with the Energy of your Source, and so you have no real value to give; and second, your attention to their need only amplifies their need.

Of course, it is a wonderful thing to help others, but you must do it from your position of strength and alignment, which means you must be in alignment with their success as you offer assistance, and not in alignment with their problem.

It is easy to know if your offer is coming from a place of alignment or resistance because you can always tell by the way you are feeling. When your awareness of their situation makes you uncomfortable and you offer help to make them feel better and to make yourself feel better, you are not in the Vortex and you are not helping. *When you feel an inspired eagerness to offer something because you want to participate in their happy, successful process, your attention to their success harmonizes with the point of view of your Source; and the infinite resources of the Universe are at your disposal. And that does help.*

⋇ 8 ⋇

When you look for another's strengths,
even when they are hard to find,
your attention to them amplifies them;
and, in time, because of the spotlight you have shined,
those strengths will become apparent to others as well.

Sometimes others are so focused on the unpleasant details of their current situation that they are unable to catch even a glimpse of hope for things to turn around. Because they are so embroiled in the reality they are living, they continue to perpetuate Vibrations that match what they do not want—and so they continue to attract more of what they do not want.

But when you have been practicing your Vibration of alignment, and you are consistently inside your Vortex, you are able to see them as the successful people that they truly are rather than the people who are temporarily pinching off their success. They are often so far Vibrationally removed from the success that awaits them inside their Vortex that they are unable to find their way in; but because you are already inside the Vortex, and you are holding them as your object of attention from inside the Vortex, they are able to see you, and feel you.

That is what the power of uplifting influence really is: because you are able to recognize their true power and therefore shine a spotlight upon it, sometimes they are then able to catch a glimpse of it themselves.

Your negative attention to anything perpetuates more negative attention. Your positive attention to anything perpetuates more positive. However, your positive attention is much more influential than your negative attention, because when you align with your Source inside your Vortex—you access the power that creates worlds. *Our daily meditation process will help you to find and maintain your alignment with the Energy that creates worlds, so that you can then offer your true power of upliftment as you shine the spotlight of your gaze upon others. Literally everyone you think about from inside the Vortex benefits.*

When others lash out at you in anger,
with words or action, their battle is not with you
but with themselves; and if you do not take their
behavior personally—understanding it is their
personal battle—in time they'll leave you out of it.

It always feels good to observe another person who is feeling good; and when his or her happiness is associated with your behavior, it can feel especially good to you.

You are an uplifter, and it feels good to be a part of uplifting another. But if you encourage others to believe that their happiness is dependent upon your behavior, you are doing a very big disservice to them and to yourself. *You will eventually grow weary of attempting the impossible task of keeping others happy. For as their demands on you increase, you will lose your important sense of being free. And often, since you are the one present in their lives trying to help, when they do not feel better, they blame you.*

Everyone holds a mix of opinions, beliefs, and expectations on a myriad of subjects. When you give your attention to something, that Vibration becomes activated and comes to the forefront, so to speak; and the more often you focus upon it, and cause it to come to the forefront, the more dominant it becomes.

You have the option of making a good-feeling aspect of another person dominant in your Vibration or of making a bad-feeling aspect dominant in your Vibration, and whatever aspect you regularly choose will become the Vibrational basis of your relationship.

When your happiness becomes your highest priority, and so you deliberately keep active the best-feeling aspects of others, you will train your Vibrational frequency in such a way that they will not be able to rendezvous with you in any way that does not feel good when it happens.

The only way for anyone to be consistently happy is to understand that the feeling of happiness is simply about alignment with the Source who is within. When you are in your Vortex of Creation, you are lined up with all-that-you-have-become and with everything that you have asked for. There simply is no substitute for that alignment.

⋊ 10 ⋉

Sometimes you think it is important
what others think of you, and so you work
to extract approval from them.
However, there really is little that you can do
to keep their approval coming—for it is
never about you, but about them.

When you are children, the adults around you want you to modify your behavior in ways that please them, which sometimes does not
seem like such a bad idea from their perspective, but ultimately has
far-reaching detrimental outcomes for both the child and the adult. *It
does not work out for the one who is attempting to do the pleasing, because
there are too many people who want different things from you, and keeping up with the ever-changing ideas of what another believes is appropriate*

behavior is no small task. And it also does not work out for the one who wants to be pleased, because if you are able to get some others to modify their behavior to please you, then you are continuously needing control of others, or cooperation from others, to be pleased. An impossible and futile endeavor.

If you have developed the pattern of working hard to keep those around you happy, then when they are not happy, when they are presenting their anger to you, you may feel that their anger has something to do with your behavior. *They often work hard to make you believe that you are the primary reason for their problem, but you have undoubtedly discovered that the more you attempt to modify your behavior to keep others happy, the more modification of your behavior they seem to require. Again, an impossible and futile endeavor.*

When you demonstrate your consistent state of happiness that you are achieving by being aware of your Vortex and holding thoughts that allow your frequent entrance into it (and, even more important, you do not modify your behavior to try to soothe or solve the problems of others), you will offer them—through the power of your example—the secret to their own true happiness. Being happy is a very personal thing—and it really has nothing to do with anyone else.

If you will release all concern about
how others feel about you, and focus only
upon how you feel about them, you will unearth
your core understanding of *who-you-really-are,*
and you will discover what true freedom really is.

The current opinion that others hold regarding you has far more to do with how they are feeling (whether they are in alignment with their own Source, and whether they are in or out of their Vortex at the time) than it has to do with you or your behavior.

There is perhaps no greater waste of time and effort than that of trying to influence the way other people see you, because what they see has very little to do with their object of attention and everything to do with the vantage point from which they are looking. <u>*How others feel about you is really about their relationship with their own Vortex.*</u>

Since their good feeling is about their relationship with their *Inner Being,* or about being inside their Vortex, then your best plan of helping them to feel better is always to encourage or influence them into their Vortex. But you can only effectively do that when you are inside your own Vortex and in alignment with your own *Inner Being.*

So if you are observing others who are unhappy (for any reason), your very observation of their unhappiness prevents you from being in your Vortex—and so it is not possible for you to help them. But if, instead, your priority is being inside your own Vortex, and so you do not allow yourself to focus upon their problem or their unhappiness, and so you remain inside your Vortex . . . now, as you hold them as your object of attention from inside *your* Vortex, you may influence them to enter *their* Vortex, and therefore feel better.

True freedom is found in the absence of resistance. It is about being able to feel good and to be inside your Vortex regardless of the situations or conditions that surround you. True freedom is the discovery of maintaining unconditional love—of being able to maintain your "in the Vortex" position regardless of conditions.

≼ 12 ≽

At your core, you are more alike than different, for you
share a common thread of *Source* and *love* and *expansion.*
And so, if you feel threatened by another,
that threat is not real, for only you can stop
the flow of your natural Well-Being.

None of you take it well when you are out of alignment with your Source. The feeling of emptiness that you experience when you are disallowing your Connection to your power and Energy and clarity is extremely unpleasant. And often—when you or others are in that state of resistance—you display your disconnection by taking it out on others.

When you see anyone trying to control others, you are witnessing some-one who is outside of his or her Vortex and pinching off his or her own resources of Well-Being. This person is futilely attempting to compensate for a self-imposed denial of resources by bullying someone else.

If you allow the threatening or unpleasant behavior of others to make you feel bad, you have simply joined the chain-of-pain outside of your Vortex. We want you to understand that they hold no power over you.

Everyone wants to feel good, to be of value, to be engaged with life, to feel progress, to learn new things, and to feel love. But many people are looking for love in all the wrong places. When you witness unpleasant behavior in another, it is not so different from seeing someone with a pillow pressed to his or her face, being deprived of air to breathe. The unpleasant behavior is equivalent to him or her flailing about, desperate for life-giving air.

So just remember, when others are behaving aggressively or rudely toward you, they are simply desperate for the alignment of their Vortex. It really is not about you. It is not their threat or their seeming power or strength or position that is jeopardizing your life or your happiness. It is only your attention to something that prevents your Vibrational alignment with Source that can diminish your Well-Being—and you have complete control over that.

As you insist on looking for positive aspects in others,
in time only positive aspects can be shown to you,
for you will have incrementally adjusted your
Vibrational point of attraction;
and, by *Law*, that must be so.

Every thought that you have ever focused upon has the potential of being activated again; however, your brain is not storing all of those thoughts and then projecting them to you randomly. You are activating them because of whatever you are focused upon.

As you deliberately look for positive aspects in others who surround you, you will train your Vibrational propensity into increasing improved Vibrations. So it does not matter how many negative thoughts you have thought before, or how long you have been negatively focused. You can deliberately focus—right now—on an improved thought.

Because the *Law of Attraction* is responding to your current thought, more thoughts like that current thought are most likely to come into focus for you. In other words, the *Law of Attraction (that which is like unto itself, is drawn)* will continue to dish up for you more and more thoughts that match your current Vibrational frequency.

The more you deliberately choose better-feeling thoughts, the more easy and ready access you will have to those thoughts. But there is another fast and effective way to raise your Vibration and to put yourself in the position of having access to much better-feeling thoughts: By focusing upon your breathing, you will deactivate resistant thought. In doing so, your Vibration immediately rises until it finds resonance and alignment with the Vibration of your Source, inside your Vortex.

We teach meditation because it is actually easier, in some situations, to help you find "no thought" than to find a positive thought. . . . There is no better path to wonderful, meaningful, good-feeling relationships than the combination of a daily meditation—allowing your Vibration to find its natural balance—and the deliberate focusing upon positive aspects.

✎ 14 ✎

It is certain that you can find the relationships that you desire,
but first there is something very important that
you must do: you must become a Vibrational Match
to the qualities that you seek, because what
comes to you always matches *you*.

Often people believe finding a mate who loves them will be the answer to everything missing in their life experience. They want to find that one person who will, in essence, complete them. And almost without exception, they want that person, right here, right now!

But because we understand the *Law of Attraction* as we do, we encourage them to ease up a bit on the "right here, right now" part, for this very important reason: *If you insist on choosing a mate right now, that mate will be a Vibrational Match to how you feel right now.*

The person who comes right now will be a match to the essence of the person you are right now.

When you are feeling misunderstood or lonely or unloved, you cannot find a mate who will offer anything different to you.

If you have predominantly been noticing the absence of a wonderful relationship, the presence of a wonderful relationship cannot occur. Not right now.

If you are seeking a joyful relationship, you must become joyful first. Asking for a relationship to make you joyful is a backward approach.

If you are seeking a satisfying relationship, you must become satisfied first.

If you are seeking a relationship full of fun and great timing and excitement, you must become full of fun and great timing and excitement, first.

How you feel equals *who-you-are.* And *who-you-are* equals everything that comes to you. The powerful *Law of Attraction* insists on that.

The most accurate way to assess your chronic Vibrational offering is to pay attention to the relationships you now have. The people who are drawn to you are a perfect reflection of your chronic thoughts, how you are feeling, and your point of attraction. And you have complete control about that.

Focus on the best you can in others;
and when characteristics you want are missing,
practice seeing them anyway—for when
you practice the thoughts of the things that you desire,
they must show up in your experience. It is *Law*.

Every person with whom you interact holds a wide variety of Vibrational potential for you to choose from. And in the same way that you deliberately select the things you want to experience for lunch as you choose from the food buffet, you can choose the characteristics of the people you are interacting with as well.

Even if the majority of what others are living and feeling and being is not pleasing to you, still you have the ability to look for and find characteristics that do please you. And when you make that your common practice, you will attract increasingly better experiences to yourself from each of them.

Remember that whenever a problematic aspect of another person is coming into your focus, an equivalent solution is coming into focus as well. And even though that person may be very far away from manifesting or experiencing the solution, it is still there. It is still within reach; and with practice, you will be able to see it. *If you are determined to feel good and are therefore equally determined to stay in your own Vortex, not only will you be able to see more and more positive aspects in others, but, in time, you will inspire them to begin seeing them in themselves as well.*

When you magnify a Vibrational aspect of anything by giving your attention to it, your spotlight makes it easier for others to see it as well.

Your attention to the positive aspects in others feels good to you because it causes you to find alignment with your *Inner Being,* but it also causes you to find alignment with their *Inner Being*—with *who-they-really-are.*

By tuning to the frequency of your Source through our daily meditation, you will have access only to the best of everyone you meet. There is no greater gift that you can give to others than the gift of recognizing them as they really are.

❖ 16 ❖

You are doing extremely well.
The relationships that you seek are flowing to you.
Relax and enjoy the unfolding. . . . Feel appreciation
for *what-is*, and eagerness for what is coming. . . .
There is great love here for you.

And, as always, we remain—in the Vortex.

You have come forth into this physical time-space reality with billions of other humans, understanding the immense value that you offer to each other and to *All-That-Is*. The splendor and richness of the relationships that you will find with others with whom you share this planet hinges completely on the relationship that you deliberately foster between the physical you and your Non-Physical counterpart, your *Inner Being*.

Your *Inner Being* demonstrates a never-ending willingness to continue seeing only your value and goodness, holding that Vibration as a place-marker for you whenever you are ready to align with it. Seeing you there even when you do not see it.

We take enormous pleasure in offering these *Law*-based, Universal concepts to you in a logical presentation, because we know the pleasure you will find when you discover your pure resonance with them.

We also take enormous pleasure in understanding that there is nothing in all of the Universe more natural than for you to feel good, and that none of the words that we have offered here in this book are necessary in order for you to bring that about.

If the only decision that we have inspired (as a result of the written and recorded message that we have offered here) is that you sit each day, for 15 minutes only, while breathing to the rhythm of the music—focusing softly, with the intention of blending your breaths, one by one, with the tempo of the music in the background—that will be enough. Enough for you to release all resistance, all discomfort, all illness, all loneliness, all unwantedness . . . as you feel that being replaced, breath by breath, with the clarity, vitality, ease, flow, and love of your Source within you.

There is great love here for you!

About the Authors

#1 *New York Times* best-selling authors **Esther** and **Jerry Hicks** produce the Leading Edge Abraham-Hicks teachings on the *Art of Allowing* our natural Well-Being to come forth. For more than two decades, their *Law of Attraction* workshops, held in up to 60 cities per year, have continued to inspire a regular flow of Abraham books, CDs, and DVDs. Their internationally acclaimed Website is: **www.abraham-hicks.com**.

Jerry and Esther Hicks began disclosing their amazing Abraham experience to a handful of close business associates in 1986. Recognizing the practical results being received by themselves and by those people who were asking meaningful questions regarding the application of the principles of the *Law of Attraction* to finances, bodily conditions, and relationships—and then successfully applying Abraham's answers to their own situations—Jerry and Esther made a deliberate decision to allow the Teachings of Abraham® to become available to an ever-widening circle of seekers of answers to how to live a better life.

And so, since 1989, using their San Antonio, Texas, conference center as their base, Esther and Jerry have traveled to approximately 50 cities a year (throughout Australia, Canada, England, Ireland, and the United States), presenting a series of interactive *Law of Attraction* Workshops to those leaders who have gathered to participate in this progressive stream of thought. And although worldwide attention has been given to this philosophy of Well-Being by Leading Edge thinkers and teachers who have, in turn, incorporated many of Abraham's revolutionary concepts into their best-selling books, scripts, lectures, films, and so forth, the primary spread of this material has been from person to person, as individuals begin to discover the value of applying this learnable-teachable form of spiritual practicality to their personal life experiences.

Abraham—a group of obviously evolved Non-Physical teachers— speak to us through Esther. And as they speak to our level of comprehension through a series of loving, allowing, brilliant, yet comprehensively simple essays in print and in sound, they guide us to a clear Connection with our loving, guiding *Inner Being* and to uplifting self-empowerment from our Total Self.

Featuring the concept of the Universal *Law of Attraction,* the Hickses have published more than 800 Abraham-Hicks books, cassettes, CDs, and DVDs that have been translated into more than 30 different languages. They may be contacted through their extensive interactive Website at: **www.abraham-hicks.com**; or by mail at Abraham-Hicks Publications, P.O. Box 690070, San Antonio, TX 78269.

Hay House Titles of Related Interest

YOU CAN HEAL YOUR LIFE, the movie, starring Louise L. Hay & Friends
(available as a 1-DVD program and an expanded 2-DVD set)
Watch the trailer at: **www.LouiseHayMovie.com**

THE SHIFT, the movie,
starring Dr. Wayne W. Dyer
(available as a 1-DVD program and an expanded 2-DVD set)
Watch the trailer at: **www.DyerMovie.com**

ANGEL THERAPY® MEDITATIONS, by Doreen Virtue (CD)

ANGEL WORDS: Visual Evidence of How Words Can Be Angels in Your Life,
by Doreen Virtue and Grant Virtue (book)

CHANGE YOUR THOUGHTS MEDITATION: Do The Tao Now!
by Dr. Wayne W. Dyer (CD)

MEDITATIONS FOR MANIFESTING: Morning and Evening Meditations to Literally Create Your Heart's Desire, by Dr. Wayne W. Dyer (CD)

MEDITATIONS TO HEAL YOUR LIFE, by Louise L. Hay (book)

THE POWER OF JOY: How the Deliberate Pursuit of Pleasure Can Heal Your Life,
by Christiane Northrup, M.D. (CD)

All of the above are available at your local bookstore,
or may be ordered by contacting Hay House (see last page).

We hope you enjoyed this Hay House book. If you'd like to receive our online catalog featuring additional information on Hay House books and products, or if you'd like to find out more about the Hay Foundation, please contact:

Hay House, Inc., P.O. Box 5100, Carlsbad, CA 92018-5100
(760) 431-7695 or (800) 654-5126
(760) 431-6948 (fax) or (800) 650-5115 (fax)
www.hayhouse.com® • **www.hayfoundation.org**

⁂

Published and distributed in Australia by: Hay House Australia Pty. Ltd., 18/36 Ralph St., Alexandria NSW 2015 • *Phone:* 612-9669-4299 • *Fax:* 612-9669-4144 • www.hayhouse.com.au

Published and distributed in the United Kingdom by: Hay House UK, Ltd., 292B Kensal Rd., London W10 5BE • *Phone:* 44-20-8962-1230 • *Fax:* 44-20-8962-1239 • www.hayhouse.co.uk

Published and distributed in the Republic of South Africa by: Hay House SA (Pty), Ltd., P.O. Box 990, Witkoppen 2068 • *Phone/Fax:* 27-11-467-8904 • www.hayhouse.co.za

Published in India by: Hay House Publishers India, Muskaan Complex, Plot No. 3, B-2, Vasant Kunj, New Delhi 110 070 • *Phone:* 91-11-4176-1620 • *Fax:* 91-11-4176-1630 • www.hayhouse.co.in

Distributed in Canada by: Raincoast, 9050 Shaughnessy St., Vancouver, B.C. V6P 6E5 • *Phone:* (604) 323-7100 • *Fax:* (604) 323-2600 • www.raincoast.com

⁂

Take Your Soul on a Vacation

Visit **www.HealYourLife.com®** to regroup, recharge, and reconnect with your own magnificence.Featuring blogs, mind-body-spirit news, and life-changing wisdom from Louise Hay and friends.

Visit **www.HealYourLife.com** today!